Reflections
LIVING
Right-Side Up in an Upside-Down World

Mark and Dallas Henslee

Published by
Blue Fire Legacy
Westcliffe, Colorado

Unless otherwise indicated, all Scripture quotations are from the ESV© Bible (The Holy Bible, English Standard Version©), copyright © 2001 by Crossway, a publishing ministry of Good News Publishers. Used by permission. All rights reserved.

NIV–THE HOLY BIBLE, NEW INTERNATIONAL VERSION®, NIV® Copyright ©1973, 1978, 1984, 2011 by Biblica, Inc.™ Used by permission. All rights reserved worldwide.

NKJV–Scripture taken from the New King James Version®. Copyright © 1982 by Thomas Nelson. Used by permission. All rights reserved.

NLT–Scripture quotations are taken from the *Holy Bible*, New Living Translation, copyright ©1996, 2004, 2007 by Tyndale House Foundation. Used by permission of Tyndale House Publishers, Inc., Carol Stream, Illinois 60188. All rights reserved.

All works cited are used with permission.

To protect the privacy of individuals whose stories are told in this book, permission has been obtained to share the stories, or names and identifiers have been removed from the accounts.

Copyright © 2022 Mark and Dallas Henslee

Cover Design Photo: Free image by BNPDesignStudio on Canva Pro, modified Akilah Picou

Cover Layout: Dallas Henslee

Back Cover Author Photograph: Cathy Troyer

ISBN 978-0-9989548-4-4

All rights reserved. With the exception of using a short quote of 50 words or less to promote the teachings presented in this book, no part of this book may be reproduced, stored in a retrieval system, or transmitted in any form or by any means--electronic, mechanical, photocopy, recording, or otherwise-- without prior written permission of the copyright owner. All promotional quotes should provide credits including title and authors. Please direct your inquiries to info@bluefirelegacy.org.

Reflections: Living Right-Side Up in an Upside-Down World

Dedication _____ v

Preface _____ vi

God Stories: Sharing Life with Others _____ 1

Section 1 Provision and Protection

The Lord is THE Provider _____ 6

Five Truths About God's Provision _____ 13

Shielded from Destructive Crushing Waves _____ 21

Giddy Giving with God, the Gift of Generosity ____ 25

Section 2 Not of this World

Seven Lessons About Sin I Learned From a Rat ___ 31

Rotting on the Inside and Protecting Our Integrity _ 36

That's Not Really Stealing, Is It? _____ 40

Identifying the Source of the Pain _____ 46

Be Set On Fire for God's Kingdom _____ 51

Section 3 Obedience and Faith

Living Right-Side Up in an Upside-Down World ___57

From Selfish to Sacrificial Living _____63

Our Opinions Provide Comfort in the Absence of God's Perspective_____68

We Bring the Sacrifice of Praise, Service and Worship _____72

Plucking Sentimental Heart Strings to Resolve Dissonant Chords _____77

The Incredible Power of Music in Our Lives _____81

Is It Okay to Wrestle with God?_____86

Waving the Flag of Conditional Surrender _____90

Section 4 Reflecting and Light

Reflecting a Kaleidoscope of Joy and Love _____99

Walk with the Light of the World _____ 103

Shine Bright in the Darkness of the World_____ 108

Section 5 Identity Issues

The Plague of the Never-ending Finish _____ 113

Stung by the Plague of Busyness_____ 119

Bloom Where You Are Transplanted_____ 123

A Glimpse of a Father and Son and What Relationship Could Be_____ 127

Receive the Father's Unconditional Love _____ 133

Anxiety in a World of Unknowns and Confusion __ 138

Struggling to Walk in High Heels _____ 142

Today, Today is a Really Hard Day _____ 146

When Awe of the Extraordinary Fades to Common
_____ 151

Live Your Life as a Conqueror! _____ 155

Section 6 Edification and Exhortation

Thanksgiving Adventures and the Power of Words
_____ 162

Building Beautiful Sandcastles in the Church ____ 166

Using Our Brains in a World of Information and Technology _____ 170

Joined in the Fire or Cooling on the Side _____ 176

Section 7 Community and Unity

Slipping on the Hills of Life _____ 182

Living in the Desert _____ 187

Parenting Truths You Can Use in Any Relationship
_____ 192

Unity Through the Strength of Diversity _____ 197

Section 8 Rest and Restoration

Are You Pouring From a Broken Carafe?_____ 203

Restlessness in the Face of Rest_____ 207

Learning How to Rest in the Sabbath _____ 211

Just the Waterboy_____ 216

A Desert Under the Rainforest_____ 220

Section 9 Hope, Faith, and Love

Journeying From Dream to Fulfillment_____ 225

How to Find an Auto Mechanic by Listening_____ 232

When You are Lost, Look for the Avalanche _____ 236

When Free Parking Isn't So Fun_____ 241

Six Keys for Implementing Change in Your Life___ 246

The Mercy of "No" and "Not Yet" _____ 253

Planning International Travel by Prayer and Faith _____ 257

Dedication

First and foremost, we dedicate these stories to our Lord and Savior. We long to be found faithful servants of the Most High King. Secondly, we dedicate this project to our family members and friends who have walked this journey with us. May our testimonies continue to encourage you to keep your eyes above the waves and the water, fixing them on Jesus, the Author and Perfecter of your faith.

Preface

Enclosed in these pages are selected journey entries which record some of the lessons we have learned over the last several years. Mark decided he preferred "journey" over "journal" entry because it communicates the relational aspect of the Christian walk better, and so that is what we have affectionately named them. While these stories were originally posted in chronological order on the ministry's website, we have chosen to group them by topic in this collection. The goal for our writings is to share the truths we have learned along the way, and to encourage you to journey with the Lord in faith and obedience.

Consistent with our other projects, we purposely write in conversational English rather than the formal English typically deemed proper for published works. We believe the easier it is to read a topic, the easier it is to comprehend and apply the spiritual concepts in your life.

While the Christian walk is not free of hardship, it is worth the cost. Hard does not always equal bad, and hardship does not always mean you are out of God's will. Read our stories with your own in mind. What is God showing you today?

God Stories: Sharing Life with Others

"And they have conquered him by the blood of the Lamb and by the word of their testimony, for they loved not their lives even unto death." (Revelation 12:11, ESV)

Everyone enjoys stories. We watch them on TV and in the movies, read them in books, and see them in the theater. When families get together, it is common to tell stories of the past. Do you have some favorite family stories?

Our daughters and soon-to-be son (we typically skip the "in-law" portion) were all home for Christmas. As we sat around the table eating great food, we got to share life. We shared stories of the past; stories that were familiar and some new ones. With every story, the kids get to know more about their parents, and hopefully a better view of how God has worked throughout the years to grow us to where we are today.

Relationships

Stories share facts and events, but some of the best ones are really about relationship. Our lives are filled with interactions with other people. My favorite stories are about God journeying with us.

The Bible is full of stories about God walking in relationship with His creation. In Genesis, we see the Lord walking daily with Adam and Eve in the Garden of Eden. Story after story, God interacts with His children all the way through to Revelation where we see Him reclaiming the earth for all eternity.

The Lord doesn't need us, but He greatly desires us. He wants to be a part of our daily life, every moment and detail. Sometimes we get it, and other times, we completely miss Him. Through each interaction, we live a story.

Lessons

Stories can be entertaining, encouraging, enlightening, or exhilarating. In most stories, there is a lesson to be learned. Things we should or shouldn't do, ways to respond to situations, and spiritual insights of man and God.

God stories provide encouragement to keep going in our faith journey. We are able to lift each other up through our stories. I'm able to see hope where I otherwise would see despair because of what others have gone through and their willingness to share.

I'd posit that many of us are fairly good about teaching our kids Scripture, but too many of us don't talk about what God has done in our life. We aren't very good at telling our God stories. There are so many important life lessons that others need to learn from our experiences. We need to be telling about the many things that God is doing in, and through, our life. Sharing our stories will help build the faith of others and strengthen our own faith as we recount the goodness and faithfulness of God in our own life.

Tell Your Story

"Tell your children of it, and let your children tell their children, and their children to another generation." (Joel 1:3, ESV)

We often think that our story is insignificant or doesn't have enough meaning to be shared. Don't discount your story. I've found that the stories I think have less meaning, often, are the ones that have the greater impact for others.

Some of the harder stories to tell are the ones which involve my failures. It requires a willingness to look foolish in the eyes of others. That's hard. We prefer to tell about our great exploits and conquests. However, the world needs to hear the good, the bad, and the ugly.

I can probably tell more stories of failure than success. Times when I missed the mark; when I failed to hear and do what God said; when I put myself before others; when I got angry instead of showing love. I'm an imperfect man with room for improvement.

When we are willing to humble ourselves and tell about our failures, God is able to lift up others. I'm a son that is greatly loved by my Father in Heaven, and as such, I'm not a failure. Other people need to hear that they are not a failure just because they fail. They need to know the redemption of our Savior. Some will only hear about the Lord through our stories.

What God stories do you have to share with others? Find someone that you can share your stories with. God will be glorified if you are willing to tell about Him and how He has been working in your life.

Originally posted on www.bluefirelegacy.org by Mark Henslee on 03/15/19

1
Provision and Protection

The Lord is THE Provider

"Consider the ravens: they neither sow nor reap, they have neither storehouse nor barn, and yet God feeds them. Of how much more value are you than the birds!"

(Luke 12:24, ESV)

In March 2016, I was working in my makeshift office (what used to be our oldest daughter's bedroom) when the Lord spoke. There wasn't an audible voice, but it was so clear, it might as well have been.

"Mark, I am the provider."

"Yes, Lord, I know You are a good provider, and You have taken care of us over the years."

"Mark, I am the provider."

"Yes, Lord. You are our provider."

All too similar to Jesus asking Peter if he loved him, God said a third time, "Mark, I am THE Provider."

Then it hit me. He was telling me that He wasn't just a *good* provider. He was saying that He is *the one and only* provider. It was a call to live my life completely differently, in humility, submission, and dependence on Him in everything.

A Change in Identity

One of the roles and identities that I held was that of provider. Provider for myself, my wife, my kids, my employees, etc. I started working at age 12 with a paper route, and for the most part, I have had a job - or three - continually since then. I've always been a hard worker, willing to do what it took to make the money needed. I have started and run a few businesses. Never did I make a lot of money, but enough to be a decent provider.

Being a provider was something that was measurable, and I could do relatively well. As a bonus, it felt good to be a provider. I had people dependent upon me, and there is a certain ego boost that goes along with that role.

But that day, the Lord was removing part of my self-made identity. He was telling me that He, and He alone, is the provider. No longer was I to operate in that role. This was not necessarily a nice revelation. In fact, I've had to struggle through the process of releasing and increasing my dependence. The biggest struggle has probably been humility.

It has taken a few years for me to learn how to walk in complete dependence on Him. There are still days that I think I want to take back that control and be a provider again, but really, I don't.

Four New Principles to Live By

In starting Blue Fire Legacy, the Lord gave us four principles with regard to finances:

1. No debt

2. No regular employment – the ministry is to be our first priority and full-time endeavor

3. Don't charge for services

4. Don't beg

We've had various comments when telling people about these four requirements. The general response is along the lines of, "Well, that kind of puts you in a tight spot" or "Then how do you pay your bills?"

No debt

The first principle of no debt is relatively easy and comfortable. We spent the first 23 years of our marriage carrying some level of debt, and for many of those years, way too much debt. I had become a master at the zero-interest credit card game. If we wanted to buy something and didn't have the money, we could always borrow it and pay it later. Much like most Americans today.

In 2012, we started the process of paying down debt using the principles taught by Dave Ramsey. With the sale of the business in November 2015, we were able to pay off almost all of the debts that we had. The rest were paid off when we sold our house in August 2016. After years of being slaves to the lenders, we are more than happy to never go back in debt.

The uncomfortable part of no debt is the inconvenience often caused by not using a credit card. We have to be aware of how much money is in the account before pulling out the debit card to pay for things. This would be easier with a regular income and buffer funds, but in our situation - void of such, it requires more planning and great dependence on the Lord.

No regular employment

The second principle of no regular employment sounded really nice as well. Previously, we had always worked regular jobs along with ministry positions. This worked well economically since the ministries rarely paid much, if anything. The downside was having to balance a job with ministry needs and demands. To think that we could focus only on ministry was really appealing.

The reality of paying bills on a minister's salary, if one is even available to be paid, however, can be challenging. And in the early days of the ministry, there wasn't enough to keep us busy full-time. So, I would pick up handyman jobs or a consulting job here and there. This was okay as long as I made ministry appointments and tasks the priority and the jobs just filled in extra time.

As the ministry has grown and become a full-time commitment, there is no longer much room for these side jobs. There hasn't been for months, really since last fall. This means that we are more dependent on the Lord and donations to the ministry than ever before.

Don't charge

The third principle, don't charge for services, is great for marketing but does have a couple drawbacks. The first, obvious drawback, is that we don't have money coming into the ministry from the services provided. If you multiply the hours we spend counseling and coaching times a standard rate like Dallas used to charge in her private practice, it would be a substantial sum of money.

The second drawback is a concept that if people don't have anything at stake, they will be less committed to the process. We have found that this is the case with very few of the clients we have worked with over the past couple years. The reality is that those we are supposed to work with are very motivated to do the work. They may not have money at stake, but they have their mental and spiritual well-being on the line, as well as the ministries they have been called to, hanging in the balance. This is generally enough motivation.

The great part of not charging is that we get to come alongside people who have no financial means to be able to get the help otherwise. We have been told many times that if we charged they would not be able to see us.

Don't beg

The final principle, don't beg, has been the hardest. What constitutes begging? What is the difference between making a need known and begging? These are not easy answers to obtain. We (Dallas and I, as well as our board) have spent much time discussing and debating these questions without super clear answers.

I have to admit that we have violated this principle a couple times in the process of learning what it means. When we have, the response was sufficiently poor to know that we stepped out of bounds. Fortunately, the Lord is very gracious and forgiving as we stumble in our lack of understanding.

The principle of don't beg applies to money as well as engagements. Most ministries have a fundraising program and a marketing plan to get connected with the donors and recipients of their services. I don't believe that these programs are inherently bad or disallowed in Scripture, but for us, they are not allowed. We are completely dependent on the Lord to provide finances, clients, and speaking engagements. He often uses people who know us to provide the connections. Other times, He just makes it happen through what we call "Divine appointments."

Walking It Out

As we have been walking out the reality that the Lord is THE Provider, there have been many stories worth sharing. In the coming months, we will share some of the stories of His amazing provisions intertwined with our other devotional blogs. The learning process has been steep, we've stumbled a few times along the way, but we are experiencing the Lord in amazing ways. We have grown, changed, been uncomfortable, struggled, grown some more, remained uncomfortable ... Well, you get the idea.

What about you? Has the Lord spoken to you about dependence on Him? Are you willing to give up control and trust Him instead? I encourage you to walk out, in faith, whatever it is that He is directing you to do. Obedience is most often hard, but so worth it as we journey in relationship with Almighty God.

Originally posted on www.bluefirelegacy.org by Mark Henslee on 06/07/19

Five Truths About God's Provision

"And my God will supply every need of yours according to his riches in glory in Christ Jesus." (Philippians 4:19, ESV)

We Americans have a mentality towards "get rich quick" schemes and instant gratification. I've often called us the microwave generation because we don't have patience to wait for much and expect everything to be done quickly. Since God is more interested in our journey with Him than in the destination (i.e., our goals), I've found that He likes to take the scenic roads instead of the direct route. This characteristic translates into how He chooses to provide.

The Lord promises to provide for all of our needs (Philippians 4:19). However, He doesn't always provide in the manner we expect or would like Him to provide. There are plenty of preachers speaking a prosperity gospel that is appealing but not Scriptural. There are also preachers that share a poverty message which I don't find to be Biblical.

When looking at the story of Elijah in 1 Kings 17, we see several lessons on provision.

1. We need to be obedient.

The Lord directed Elijah where to go to receive His provision. Had Elijah chosen to argue with God and tell Him a "better" way, we would have a different story to read; probably one more similar to the Israelites wandering in the desert for 40 years. In verse 5 and again in verse 10, we see Elijah being obedient and doing what the Lord instructed. We don't see a debate or discussion of why go to these illogical places. Elijah simply obeyed. Likewise, we need to be willing to obey the Lord's commands and instructions even when they don't make sense or are uncomfortable.

2. The Lord may use unusual methods for our provision.

In verses 2-7, Elijah hangs out by a brook in a ravine being fed by ravens. Not exactly typical, even for a prophet. Then in verses 8-16, Elijah is instructed to go into enemy territory to be fed by a widow who has nothing even to feed herself. It would make much more sense for him to go to a rich Israelite family, but that is not how the Lord chose to work in this situation.

For those who think that Elijah was on a vacation for three and a half years, I challenge you to reconsider. Many of us might consider sitting by a brook with food being brought to us a nice relaxing time. And yes, that is likely the case *except* when you are hiding from a king who wants to kill you; you don't have a home to go back to; and you aren't sure what the next day will look like. Consider also the kind of food a raven would likely bring.

While we were homeless in 2016, we spent about ten weeks camping in the mountains of Colorado. We had numerous people make comments about how nice it would be to spend the days listening to the breeze through the trees, reading a book, hiking in the forest and generally enjoying the beauty and solitude of our location. Many years earlier our mom named those 40 wonderful acres "The Haven" for good reason.

However, when you are homeless; all of your remaining possessions are in storage in various locations; you have to haul in water (and thus highly conserve usage); you don't have dependable electricity; there is minimal to no cell phone coverage or internet; you're not sure when or where you are going next; and winter is approaching, things aren't so idealistic and pleasant.

3. Sometimes we have to move to see the Lord's provision.

Then, the brook ran dry.

Elijah could have thrown a big temper tantrum about how God had made him hide and now what little he had was taken away. Elijah could have postured his heart into thinking that "this is not fair, or right, or just, or the way it should be because I am worthy of better treatment."

But isn't that attitude what we often have when we get comfortable with a situation? Change is hard, even good change. But change is often required for us to grow and experience the fullness of the Lord and His provision.

When the brook ran dry, the Lord gave Elijah instructions regarding where to go for the continuation of His provision. Elijah had to get up and move in obedience (remember lesson one). Sometimes, to be obedient, you have to leave your current location or assignment and enter into a new one.

Without moving, Elijah would not have been able to receive the Lord's provision through the widow. The same applies to us today. When the Lord provided a house for Dallas and me to live in for the winter, it was easy to get comfortable in that provision. However, there came a time when we had to move for the next provision. In our case, we didn't know where we were moving, so we proceeded to put all our stuff back in storage and packed a few suitcases to become homeless, again. This time, however, we didn't go back to live at the Haven. Instead, we lived in other people's homes, similar to Elijah moving into the widow's house.

Does God provide in the same ways?

Since we couldn't stay where we were as that provision ran out (the brook ran dry so to speak), we needed to trust God to provide in another place and manner. Too often, we get comfortable and become unwilling to move as the Lord instructs. He has great provision waiting for us; that provision requires we release the past and move into the current provision. We also need to accept that He chooses to provide in a variety of ways. Just because He did so one way in the past, doesn't mean that we'll ever see provision in that same manner again.

We've experienced the Lord provide in so many different ways that we could probably write a book about all the stories. One time, He used insurance proceeds from a hail storm to provide as much money as I had paid for the vehicle just a few months earlier - and I got to keep the car (still driving it several years later)! Another time, many years ago, we had a couple show up at the door with bags of groceries. Unbeknownst to them, we had been praying for enough food to feed our kids. They brought enough that Dallas and I got to eat also! In the ministry, there have been numerous occasions where people send funds that are just what we are needing that month. We know it is the Lord putting it on their hearts to write those checks, and they do so out of obedience to Him. Other times, a job comes along at the right time, with the right profit to cover what we need.

4. The Lord's provision is always enough.

We see in verses 14-16 the promise and fulfillment that there was always enough flour and olive oil in the containers. This wasn't a natural event. Flour and olive oil don't just keep multiplying as they are used to make bread. Somehow, the Lord kept the containers replenished much like He multiplied the loaves and fish to feed the five thousand and the four thousand in the Gospels.

We are not told that the widow added a storeroom to her house for the Lord's provision either. It was a daily walk of faith, where provision came as the food was needed.

How many times have we waited for the full provision to be there before we start walking forward in the assignment?

We quote verses like Luke 14:28 to say that we need to calculate the cost and be sure we can complete the work before starting. Instead, we need to be quoting Matthew 6:11, "Give us this day our daily bread."

"Faith is the confidence that what we hope for will actually happen; it gives us assurance about things we cannot see." (Hebrews 11:1, NLT). Walking in faith requires that we move forward as the Lord instructs even when we don't see the provision ahead of time. Sometimes (dare I say MANY times), we are asked to be "foolish" in the eyes of the world (1 Corinthians 1:18-25) as we walk in faith.

When God asks us to live lives of foolishness.

As Dallas and I are currently walking out our faith journey, we are living a life of "foolishness". Logic, as dictated by social norms, says we need to abandon the ministry, or at least put it on the back burner, and get jobs so we can have money to pay the bills. While working is an option, and happening, the ministry must continue to be our first priority as that is what the Lord has instructed us to do.

During our year of homelessness, we were presented with the choice to order the printed copies of our first book *Behind Enemy Lines: A Discipleship Course in Spiritual Warfare* or use the money to pay for living expenses. So what did we do?

We ordered the books, leaving $1.27 in the account.

The next week, the Lord provided what was needed to pay that week's bills. Later that month, we had about $20 in checking and $8 in savings, and were not sure how to buy gas or food.

But the Lord provided. Since choosing to be obedient, we haven't had much money, but the bills have always been paid (though not always *when* or *how* I desired).

A side note for those who hear about us being homeless and envision us sleeping in a car or under a bridge: We were not living in poverty, though we didn't, and still don't, have much. As we continue to walk in obedience, we have not missed a meal, nor slept in anything other than a bed (though not always a comfortable one), nor had to beg for food or money.

We are children of the King of kings, and He has provided for our needs and even a few wants. That's not to say it has been easy, but the journey has been good.

5. It is really not about us.

Do you recall what the widow was doing when Elijah first met her? The widow was preparing their last meal so that she and her son could then die of starvation (Verse 12). Sometime later, the boy does die from an illness, but as the Lord desired, he was brought back to life. When the widow's son died, Elijah could have offered condolences and wept with the widow. Instead, he did the unnatural and cried out to the Lord who brought the boy back to life.

In effect, Elijah coming into the widow's house brought life for her and her son not just once but twice. And the end result was God's glory. That is what it is really all about anyway - glorifying God and loving other people.

It is easy for us to expect God to provide for us in a manner that we *like*. Fortunately, He sees what is best and provides in ways that are for His glory and benefit other people. For example, we were asked to assist two different families in ways that we are not gifted or necessarily enjoy. My first human response (internally at least), was along the lines of "No, no way, not going to happen, find someone else, this isn't my gifting, I'm not good at that, ask me to do something else, why did you even ask that of me, who do you think I am, are you nuts?"

After serving outside our gifting, while not something I would normally choose to do and it did require God's grace to flow through and over me, I enjoyed being able to see the difference that it made for those we served. Oh, and it provided money to buy the things we needed in one case and a temporary place to live in the other!

The Big Takeaway

As we walk in obedience and faith, the Lord is our Provider. He works in amazing, crazy, and sometimes [seemingly] foolish ways. He asks us to step outside our comfort zones and go places we wouldn't normally go. The result is that He is glorified, others are helped and we have what we need and some wants. I stand in awe of His incredible ways!

Originally posted on www.bluefirelegacy.org by Mark Henslee on 07/20/18

Shielded from Destructive Crushing Waves

"When you pass through the waters, I will be with you; and when you pass through the rivers, they will not sweep over you. When you walk through the fire, you will not be burned; the flames will not set you ablaze."

(Isaiah 43:2, NIV)

You know those days when you feel like one more crashing wave may cause your proverbial boat to shatter into a thousand pieces? The days when you've been riding the waves so long, you've become seasick? I've had more than a few of those in the course of life and ministry.

In those instances, whether short-lived days or extended seasons, there are spiritual reminders that the circumstances are not beyond God's control. There are Scriptures, illustrations, and life experiences which people share as encouragement.

You Are Covered

One of these encouraging words came during an intense time of sifting and training. "You will hear and feel the war raging around you. Weapons and fire will land very near you, so near that you can feel it, but it will not touch you. You are covered, you are *both* covered by God's shield."

The Lord gave the following promise directly to Israel, but it is so similar in quality to the above word of encouragement that He spoke over me through a friend, that I have personalized this promise.

"When you pass through the waters, I will be with you; and when you pass through the rivers, they will not sweep over you. When you walk through the fire, you will not be burned; the flames will not set you ablaze." (Isaiah 43:2, NIV)

The Israelites had to put faith into action to walk through the parted waters. They were not immediately transported to the other side (Exodus 14).

The three captured men, renamed Shadrach, Meshach, and Abednego by their captors, had to walk out their convictions even to the point of facing what appeared to be certain death in the furnace, yet they were not burned, nor did they smell of smoke when they came out of the furnace (Daniel 3).

Walking Through Water and Fire

We have been asked to pass through the water and fire. Over the last 20 years, we've left a home church family that we loved and partner tracks in both our places of employment to move from Texas to Colorado to help church plant (aka start a new church). The move was drastic as we had 3 small children, no jobs, no housing, and the sale of our house fell through right before we left. The church plant we relocated to assist closed within four short months.

After a time, history somewhat repeated, and Mark walked away from a lucrative position (again being on partner track) to start his own firm and have more scheduling flexibility to be a bi-vocational pastor of a church plant. Several years later, we found ourselves in a forced exit due to a power play rather than a disciplinary action. Our ministry, our home church, our friends, and our support structure went "Poof!" all at once.

We've been reprimanded by church and denominational leaders for following God's way instead of man's. We've endured the additional difficulties of family life, strained finances, etc. that come with being in active ministry, and we've even had a time where God did not restore us to formal ministry. Restoration and sending us back out came with the price of releasing our man-made identities and imaginary box of who God was to us, defined solely and incorrectly, by us.

Leave Your Nets

Remember when Jesus was walking on the shore and said, "Leave your nets and come follow Me" (Matthew 4:18-22; Mark 1:16-20)? He asked the same of us. We closed our businesses, turned away from our security in our professions, sold much of what we owned, and paid off all the debt we had incurred; doing so necessitated being homeless for a year. Choosing to live, minister, and develop a ministry from scratch while remaining completely debt-free has not been easy. There were, and still are, days that it feels that the circumstances or due dates can overwhelm us. Sometimes we come right down to the wire of needing a provision whether it be food, money to pay a bill, or plane tickets. We have the promise that we will not be overcome, and so we continue to walk through.

Promise of Passage

See, the promise that was given to us didn't say we would be removed from the war, just like the promise given to Israel didn't remove the obstacles. It says, "I will be with you." In other words, *I will see you through*, not *around*. *I will be your Protector, Trainer, and Sustainer.*

> *"When you go through deep waters,*
> *I will be with you.*
> *When you go through rivers of difficulty,*
> *you will not drown.*
> *When you walk through the fire of oppression,*
> *you will not be burned up;*
> *the flames will not consume you.*
> *For I am the Lord, your God,*
> *the Holy One of Israel, your Savior."*
> *(Isaiah 43:2-3a, NLT)*

Likewise, on those days, weeks, months, or years that just one more wave might send your boat toppling or dash it against the jagged rocks, God, My God, the Holy One of Israel is right there with me, and He will be there for you. I find it is so much easier to endure the hardship when my focus is on Him as He walks through the storm with us.

Originally posted on www.bluefirelegacy.org by Dallas Henslee on 08/16/19

Giddy Giving with God, the Gift of Generosity

"Each one must give as he has decided in his heart, not reluctantly or under compulsion, for God loves a cheerful giver." (2 Corinthians 9:7, ESV)

Have you ever noticed that when we have something taken away that the importance of it increases? Some of us enjoy being around people and socializing. The past three months we've been living in a weird world of social distancing and the pleasure of hanging out with people has been greatly hindered. Zoom calls are not the equivalent of being in the same room with someone. When we miss something, it becomes more precious.

One Sunday morning, I was just giddy as I wrote our tithe check. I definitely met the definition of a cheerful giver that day. You see, we had several weeks in a row with no income, and therefore, no tithe to give. It struck me just how much I missed giving and the joy that it brings to give back to the Lord.

We generally tithe each week on that week's income. While we should always be giving cheerfully, when the opportunity is taken away, it becomes that much more important to us.

An Act of Worship

Many Christians today don't want to talk about giving because somewhere along the line they were manipulated or guilted into giving instead of being taught the truth about our finances. What a grievous position to be placed in by a leader of the church.

The truth is, giving to God is to be an act of worship. The amount isn't as important as the heart of worshiping the Lord by giving back a portion of our possessions to Him. I don't give because I have to or because I expect something in return. I give because I love and adore my Lord.

Dallas likes flowers. She knows when I buy flowers for her if it was to make up for a mistake, an attempt to gain her affection through the purchase, out of obligation because of the date on the calendar, or if it was simply an act of love. Regardless of my motivation, she will receive the flowers. However, when she feels my love in the gift, she cherishes the gift and the giver (me), more. Motivation matters.

As we give, the Lord knows our motivation. When we give out of our love for Him, there is a sweet fragrance in the offering. He is able to receive the gift with pleasure, and we, in turn, have great joy in the giving.

Owners or Stewards

We like to think that we own stuff, and the more stuff that we own, the happier we will be. My experience has been that when I thought I owned something, it generally owned me. The house requires maintenance, the car eats money for gas and repairs, the toys don't seem as fun as they used to be. The stuff that I thought would make me happy might bring temporary pleasure, but eventually requires more from me, degrades, or loses its appeal until it ends up just another thing.

There is a house that has my name on the title of it; a car and bank accounts that legally show me as the owner. Stuff that I call mine. But the truth is, I'm really a steward of these things and not the true owner.

As a steward, I view things differently. It's like being a manager of a business. I want to do my best to take care of my boss's business. I strive to succeed and am careful with the decisions I make. I'll talk with the owner to find out what He wants me to do in each situation that I haven't previously received instructions. His best interest is my first thought.

Hard work is important, but don't think that because you work hard you've earned all that you receive. The Lord's hand of blessing is far greater than we could ever achieve through hard work. When we acknowledge the Lord's ownership over our time and possessions, we are able to shift from owner to steward. We are the instruments that the Lord chooses to use to supply all of the needs for those who belong to Him and those who are searching for Him.

Freedom to Give

Since we don't really own what passes through our bank accounts, it is really easy to give as the Lord directs. In fact, we get to be a part of His blessing for others, and that brings us joy and pleasure.

Over the years, we've had fun figuring out how to get gift cards and cash to someone without them knowing where it came from. Whether that was to drop it into a woman's purse, hide it in a place they would find it at their house, or various other ways, we've anonymously been the instrument for God's provision and blessing for someone in need.

Recently, we were impressed to give some money to help feed starving pastors in a third world country. God arranged the connections to the ones in need. We got the joy of knowing that these pastors would be able to eat in the midst of lack.

We've also learned how to be the recipient of the Lord's provision and blessing through other's gifts. The Lord truly gives good things - and He uses people (you and me) to facilitate most of the transactions.

A Cheerful Giver

Who owns your bank accounts and things? Are you able to freely give and receive as the Lord directs and experience the joy of walking in financial obedience? Do you miss giving if the opportunity is removed from you for a time? Do you give joyfully without obligation but out of love?

I haven't always been a cheerful giver. It used to be an act of obligation instead of worship. Having learned to be a steward instead of owner, I've experienced great joy in giving. I pray that you will also be able to experience that same joy as you journey with the Lord in your finances. May you be giddy as you give!

"Each one must give as he has decided in his heart, not reluctantly or under compulsion, for God loves a cheerful giver. And God is able to make all grace abound to you, so that having all sufficiency in all things at all times, you may abound in every good work." (2 Corinthians 9:7-8, ESV)

Originally posted on www.bluefirelegacy.org by Mark Henslee on 06/19/20

2
Not Of This World

Seven Lessons About Sin I Learned From a Rat

Everyone who sins is breaking God's law, for all sin is contrary to the law of God. And you know that Jesus came to take away our sins, and there is no sin in Him.

(1 John 3:4-5, NLT)

One night, I heard something fall in the corner of the room – it was a jar lid, but what made it fall? I thought it was a mouse as it scurried along the top of the wall ledge. "What is available to get rid of this creature that I don't want to share the house with for the night?" I wondered.

It was safely going along the two walls as there was a ledge at the top of the block and over the window. Then it slipped and fell down onto a chair. "Surely now, if I can just find something, I can get it." But being in a strange place, I didn't know what was available or the protocols for such creatures. Our host was out, and so after the mouse went under the couch that I had previously been sitting on, I decided to go sit outside.

I wasn't outside long when I heard it and looked at the screen door – it was climbing along the inside of the screen obviously wanting to get out. I went to the door and flung it open, but instead of scurrying out, it jumped back and ran under the couch.

When our host came home, I asked what she had to deal with a mouse. "A mouse? We have a mouse?" She didn't have any glue traps for mice but did have them for rats so that is what she provided. I looked at this large glue trap and thought, "What a waste." In Colorado, the mouse traps are so much smaller and work just fine. The packaging said you could cut it, so that is what I did. I cut it down to about the size of the mouse traps we use at home.

Watching the Struggle for Freedom

After supper, we came back and behold there was the mouse in the trap. It looked bigger when it was stuck and she said, "Are you sure it's a mouse and not a rat?" She also thought that we should put out the bigger part of the trap as it was working to get off the small trap.

I watched it struggle and fight to free itself from the glue. What a battle. It would work for a while and then take a break. I placed the larger glue trap next to it, so that as it fought from the one, it would be stuck to the other.

In the morning, I went to see if it was dead. Sure enough, it had worked its way off of the small trap and was completely on the big one. Stuck. And still. Trapped. Never to scurry again.

I learned seven lessons about sin from this rat:

1. When we walk along the edge of life, it is easy to slip and fall.

Just as the rat was comfortable along the wall ledge, it lost its footing and found itself in a different place than it had planned. We also can get comfortable and lose sight of where we are or where we are going and trip up. We need to be sure that our walk with the Lord is in focus so that we don't get distracted by someone or something, as that rat did. This will require a conscious effort to read and study God's Word, be aware of our shortcomings, and have a support system around us like an accountability partner.

2. We need to take advantage of the opportunity for freedom when it is presented.

Had the rat run out the door instead of back in the house, he would be living today and continuing to grow. We often are comfortable in our situation and don't take advantage of a change when we should. Don't let the status quo be all you desire. Strive for and seek the open doors that the Lord provides for us to escape, even if they are out into the dark unknown.

3. Sin is a deadly trap.

Just like that glue trap, once you get into sin, it is very difficult to get out. Each move may help us get out but may also get us stuck more. Not all sin leads to immediate death, but ultimately, the wages of sin is death (Romans 6:23). If you are stuck in sin, call out to Jesus Christ for help. He is able to free you from the trap.

4. Sin can cause us damage.

While it is possible to get free of the trap of sin, it will still have caused damage to us. Had I not placed the bigger glue trap there, the rat would have been free in due time, but he wasn't going to be the same as before. God's forgiveness erases the sin but not necessarily the consequences. For example, if you look at pornography, while there is forgiveness, you will still have to face your spouse and their hurt and disappointment.

5. Once trapped, we are hindered from what we should be doing.

While I'm not sure just what a rat should be doing (as I don't like them), I do know that fighting to get out of a glue trap is not their normal routine. As Christians, we cannot worship and serve the Lord as we should while trapped in sin. Far too many ministers have been removed from the pulpit or mission field because of moral failures. While there can be restoration, there will be a time of lost opportunity to minister.

6. A little sin may lead to a bigger problem.

A little sin may not be deadly but can slow us down such that the enemy can put a bigger temptation to sin in place. While the rat did get free from the small trap, he was caught in the big trap that led to his demise. The time of being in the small trap allowed me the opportunity to strategically place the big trap, so that it was inevitable for him to get stuck in it.

The rat's full focus was on escaping the little trap, and it did not notice the bigger trap waiting to snatch it. The enemy often gets us off track with little things – maybe it is negativity or criticism of others. He then leads us down a path of destruction. It may start with a look, then a thought, followed by a conversation, then a touch and on down the road to the affair. We need to break the chain of events at the earliest stage possible.

7. Even the big trap may not be fatal.

The part of the story that I didn't tell you is that even in the morning there was still life in the rat. While wounded and certainly not healthy, if someone had freed it from the glue, it could have lived.

Jesus paid the ultimate price to free us from the traps of our sin. There may still be consequences to our actions but death is not required from us if we repent, accept the gift of salvation and forgiveness, and walk as the redeemed children of God. Our old self is to die and we become a new creation in Christ (Romans 6:4). This gives us a new life to live in fullness of Christ's power and His purity. As Jesus said to the woman caught in adultery, "Go and sin no more." (John 8:11, NKJV)

Originally posted on www.bluefirelegacy.org by Mark Henslee on 09/07/18

Rotting on the Inside and Protecting Our Integrity

"...for we aim at what is honorable not only in the Lord's sight but also in the sight of man."

(2 Corinthians 8:21, ESV)

When we purchased our house back in 2017, we remodeled every square inch of the inside. The outside, however, has been a more drawn out process. Within the first year, I stepped down off the front deck and went all the way to the ground, through the top step. It had rotted underneath, and that day, it gave out. I replaced all of the steps but left the decks in place as they were.

Recently, I had the privilege of being able to replace the front deck boards and framing. A couple weeks before starting the project, Dallas put a heel through a deck board as we were heading out to church. I knew that there was some decay and a few really soft spots but most of it seemed okay. Obviously, what was seen from the surface was not the whole story.

Looking on the Inside

As my son (technically son-in-law) and I were pulling off the boards, we could see the extent of the decay. There were soft places in most of the boards. Some areas were almost completely rotted through.

I had hoped to keep some of the framing based on what I could see from the outside. But as we worked, we knew it wasn't going to be long before the frame was completely disintegrated. So, we kept pulling more and more apart. The entire underside needed to be replaced.

Christians are normally really good at making it appear that we are stable and secure. Many of us have some soft spots in our life, places that look like they aren't too bad, but underneath they are rotten. It takes some work to see, and it isn't a fun experience to dig down to the root.

Going to the Roots

It is not enough to put a coat of paint on the surface and make things look good. If I had stained the deck boards when we bought the house, they would have looked good, but Dallas would have still put her heel through the board.

What we need is for the Lord to come in and take the rotten decayed places and replace them with new solid material. We are often our own worst enemy in this department. We don't want anyone else to know what is on the inside. It's uncomfortable to be exposed, especially with our weaknesses. Fear and insecurity will often keep us from being vulnerable enough to get down to the bottom of our issues.

We need to dig up all of the roots of the problem for complete healing. Some of those roots may go way back to our childhood. Almost certainly, we will have some forgiveness work to do. When we complete the difficult work, we can walk in freedom. The strength of the new will be solid and firm, built on a foundation of Christ.

Maintaining the Integrity

In the spring, I will be staining the new deck boards. It will make it look better, but more importantly the stain will seal the wood and protect it from the causes of rot. In the future, the deck will need to be re-stained on a periodic basis to maintain the protection. This will keep the deck's integrity intact for the decades to come.

We need to be putting protections in our life to defend against the elements of this world that lead to rot and decay. The armor of God is a great place to start (see Ephesians 6:10-18). It's not a one-time event, rather something that we reapply regularly.

Another protection that we should consider having in our life is an accountability partner. Dallas is my best friend and confidante. However, I need a man that I can talk with, and be accountable to, in addition to my wife. Women also need to have another woman in their life that walks in a depth of relationship beyond mere friendship.

I encourage you to take a deep look at the inside of your life. Are there soft areas that need further investigation to determine if you have some rot developing? Do you have some hurts from the past that are still hanging out in the background? There is complete healing and freedom available through Christ Jesus. Are you willing to do the work needed to walk in fullness of His purity and power?

Originally posted on www.bluefirelegacy.org by Mark Henslee on 02/19/21

That's Not *Really* Stealing, Is It?

"'And you shall not steal.'" (Deuteronomy 5:19, ESV)

Several years ago, I got a phone call from Mark. It was one of those phone calls that you just know is about to deliver bad news before much, if anything, is said. Sure enough, through an odd sequence of events, he had discovered that one of his employees had been embezzling large amounts of money from a client.

He was sick. I was sick. We never would have suspected something like this from them, and now Mark had the responsibility to notify the client that had been impacted. We later found out that there was a prior history of this behavior which demonstrated that this was a heart issue not an impulse behavior because of undesirable or difficult life circumstances.

It's easy to identify embezzlement as stealing, but there are other actions that also qualify as such, while being much less obvious. Let's take a look at some of the Scriptures that deal with stealing and then we'll dive into life application of those less obvious ways we might be stealing without realizing it.

What the Bible Says About Stealing

Do not steal. It's one of the Ten Commandments (Exodus 20:15, Deuteronomy 5:19, Mark 10:19, *et al*), and there are numerous examples of discipline because this command was not followed. I've listed a few below.

- There is the story of Achan. The Israelite army suffered defeat, and Achan, his family, and all he owned were killed because he stole from God. (Joshua 6:18-19, 7:1,10-26)
- How about Jonah? He was going to steal the ability to be reconciled with God from all the people of Nineveh by not going and prophesying, which was ultimately delivering the message which resulted in repentance, as God instructed him. (Jonah 1:1-7)
- One could be crucified for stealing just as the two thieves that hung on either side of Christ. (Matthew 27:38)
- Then there were the money changers and merchants in the Temple who were robbing people. (Mark 11:15-17)

Stealing is a Heart Issue

Stealing was, and is, a serious offense. The Bible says theft is a heart issue. Theft, amongst other offenses, comes out of our heart and can dishonor a person. The person with a right heart seeks to not offend a neighbor; to love their neighbor as themselves (Matthew 15:19 and Romans 13:9-10). In other words, to "look to the interest of others" as quoted in Philippians 2:3-4, see below.

Paul offers instructions for those that are in the habit of stealing. "Let the thief no longer steal, but rather let him labor, doing honest work with his own hands, so that he may have something to share with anyone in need" (Ephesians 4:28, ESV).

What constitutes stealing? Generally, an accepted definition is that stealing is taking anything that belongs to another by force or deceit; taking something not rightfully yours without any intent to return it. We'll look at stealing in the context of this definition; however, consider that stealing can also happen in the context of omission or refusal to acknowledge talents and gifts.

"Do nothing from selfish ambition or conceit, but in humility count others more significant than yourselves. Let each of you look not only to his own interests, but also to the interests of others." (Philippians 2:3-4, ESV)

So, What is Stealing?

Stealing is easy to identify when we think in terms of physical items: a candy bar, money, property, etc. It goes beyond that, though. How about intellectual property, plagiarism, time, someone's reputation, opportunity? The list could go on.

I've held a strong stance on stealing *opportunity*, especially in the context of operating in one's calling and spiritual gifting, for quite some time now. It's just one of those things that gets me fired up!

Too many American churches have deemed branding and packaging or image and convenience higher priority than training up the body of Christ. Does that surprise you? I see the tainting of this attitude and value across denominations and church sizes, whether they are large, multi/satellite campus churches, or small churches. And, sadly, when I was less mature in my Christian walk, I perpetrated it, but it's wrong.

We tend to like control ... even in our churches. We like to control the schedule because of our specific agenda, the next service start time, getting people out on time for the afternoon football game, or lunch (you know that friendly competition to get your congregation to the restaurants before the official "rush"). We control who can serve in which roles, based on gender or status rather than spiritual maturity and qualifications.

Stealing by Design

The problem is, while we're busy controlling all these variables, we have the audacity to pray and ask the Lord to have His way, to meet with us, to pour out His Spirit. These are all things that I believe God wants to do, and yet the unspoken part of that prayer is so limiting.

Too often, what we are really praying is more in line with something like this. "Heavenly Father, come meet with us, *but please, show up only during this brief scheduled time.*" "Holy Spirit, pour out your Spirit, *but don't interrupt the planned service, and don't do anything that might draw attention or make anyone uncomfortable.*" "Jesus, make me more like you, *but don't ask me to give up my influence or place of position that I enjoy so that I can instead wash feet, and please, Jesus, please, don't replace me with the younger/older generation!*"

How pious and selfish. God designed the Church to be a complementary body, not a family filled with selfish sibling rivalry. When we feel insecure or threatened, we can rob someone of an opportunity to grow and serve. They may not be mature enough to be in a leadership role, but that doesn't mean we should exclude them simply because we've been doing it longer or we can do it "better." We shouldn't exclude them because that "office" we hold has become our identity (aka an idol) and we just don't want to give it up. We are to edify each other and sharpen each other with teachings of the faith, testimonies of God's work in and through us, and with our spiritual gifts.

Stealing from God

The budding preacher or evangelist that is never given time in the pulpit to preach, and thereby learn by doing, is greatly handicapped. The instrumentalist or vocalist that is deemed less desirable because they are older or have less "stage presence" is denied an opportunity to lead others in worship. In more charismatic churches, we do not typically provide a safe space for those with the gift of prophecy or interpretation because someone might get it wrong, but we've taken away the place for them to learn to get it right. Worship flags, prophetic art, dance ... all of these expressions need to be celebrated and safeguarded. There are appropriate boundaries in corporate worship (see 1 Corinthians 14:26-33). Hiding them, however, is not a safeguard; it's denial of an opportunity to learn how to use one's gifting.

If we take this a step further, we are not only stealing from the individual(s), but we are stealing from The Creator that delights in His children and receives their praise and worship. Let's take that ripple effect even further. *How about the fact that we can steal the blessing God intended for those around the individual to receive? We can steal by being silent and not sharing God's truth. Remember Jonah? We can also steal by silencing someone God appointed and wants to use to impact others.*

Remember, God looks not at the outward appearance but at the heart. We need to be very careful not to let discernment turn into a practice of personal bias or unholy judgment. So, when you consider stealing in a broader sense, have you stolen from someone? If so, ask God to forgive you, to show you how to seek restoration, and prepare your heart to be willing to give someone else an opportunity.

Originally posted on www.bluefirelegacy.org by Dallas Henslee on 09/21/18

Identifying the Source of the Pain

"Strive for peace with everyone, and for the holiness without which no one will see the Lord. See to it that no one fails to obtain the grace of God; that no "root of bitterness" springs up and causes trouble…."

(Hebrews 12:14-15, ESV)

A few weeks ago, I woke up with a pain in my back such that I could hardly move. When I mustered up enough gumption to try, the pain was excruciating and brought me to tears. I woke Mark because it was abundantly obvious that something was wrong and I needed help.

As I worked through all the possible questions and causes, I considered things like:

Is this muscular or skeletal?

Did I sleep in a position that created a kink?

Did I sit too long in one place for work?

Did I pick up something incorrectly?

Is it chronic stress?

The most likely option seemed to be stress, but I wasn't sure why that was impacting my spine so negatively.

It did abate after a few days, but I had a subsequent flare and was talking to someone about it. As we talked, both of us relayed to the other that our aches and pains can often originate from another source than the point where we are noticing the ache or pain in the moment.

Looking for Roots

This pattern is true with our clients and the work they do in counseling sessions with us, as well. While the ministry scope of Blue Fire Legacy is multifaceted, a large majority of our time currently is spent talking with ministers all over the world, as we work together to identify the roots of the issues that they find distressing.

It is common to find several emotional hurts that are joined or fused together. However, we have to deal with each incident identified, not simply the most recent, for our clients to walk into healing and freedom. Usually, we discover that the pain started long before the present-day problems.

The most frequent issue is unforgiveness; however, we find that roots needing to be addressed are varied, often involving more than a single event. Much like the pain in my back, unforgiveness left unchecked will start to negatively impact areas outside of the epicenter, and the unaddressed emotional and spiritual attachments can create residual but unwanted pain.

Addressing the Correct Issue

Seeing a troublesome area while not identifying the root issue can also be true in church bodies. One can notice awkwardness or discord and be unable to identify a source. It is also possible to partially identify the problem by acknowledging disunity or tension, but only identify the current day issue, without discovering the initiation point. This is detrimental to the health of the church, and the individuals that comprise it, as the problem is likely to return.

Sometimes, what is necessary for correction is a boundary adjustment or implementation, other times conflict resolution, and still others, formal church discipline is required. In each of these circumstances, you will uncover a pattern of behavior or relational engagement. Simply addressing the current is to continually address only the symptoms of the base issue that remains disguised or covered.

If there is a pattern of rebellion to authority, manipulation, or control struggles, it is imperative to follow the chain of events back to their origin. This reminds me of the story in Joshua 7 where one man, Achan, had gone against God's instructions and the entire camp was paying the price for his disobedience. Achan was eventually found out and was put to death for his disobedience, but the matter had to be sought out. Joshua didn't only seek after God as to the reason for a swift change from victory to defeat, but for what caused the Lord to remove His protection.

Sin in the Camp

As our country is in chaos from lockdowns, riots, curfews, etc., the church has sin in the camp. We cannot get healthy until we address the roots.

Churches have not loved well. We have become inward and number focused. We have not been faithful ambassadors of the Lord's Kingdom. Instead, we have gathered around common ground, whether that be music preference, level of liturgy present, or beautiful buildings, and allowed preferences to divide the family of God. We may not be throwing physical bricks or landing assaulting blows, but we hurl hurtful words which can do equal, but hidden, damage as we scramble to "protect and defend" our positions.

For those looking from the outside in, it is no wonder they don't want to become a part of what we represent. The duplicity of behaving one way in church and another for the remaining hours of the week has to be repelling. They watch us as we are more concerned about our comfort than meeting the needs of orphans, widows, the sick, and poor. They see no difference in our lifestyle. Statistics support their claims as the percentages of those struggling with pornography and adultery fall within the same range whether evaluated with a group of professing Christians or the unchurched.

We have believed and agreed to the accusation that we are exercising unholy judgment simply by calling right right and wrong wrong based on Biblical directives. In doing so, we no longer speak the truth in love, but rather avoid conflict at all costs.

We can no longer turn a blind eye, abdicating our role as the Church. Just like the cloak, silver, and gold that were so tempting for Achan, we have brought back secular justification and rationalization (aka prohibited plunder) out of a desire for ease.

Heal Our Land

While what I noticed was an intense pain in my spine every single time I attempted to move or slightly change position, the issue was the supporting muscles which were knotted up and pulling on my spine due to unreleased, built-up stress. Treating the source rather than the symptom was what was required for relief.

Much like the Israelites, we have neglected the ways of the Lord and His instructions. We, the Church, need to repent of our sin and humble ourselves before the Lord. He is the Hope for our nation and the world. The world needs the Church to change its ways so that the land may be healed. Everything else is just dealing with a symptom instead of the root issue.

"When I shut up the heavens so that there is no rain, or command the locust to devour the land, or send pestilence among my people, if my people who are called by my name humble themselves, and pray and seek my face and turn from their wicked ways, then I will hear from heaven and will forgive their sin and heal their land." (2 Chronicles 7:13-14, NIV)

Originally posted on www.bluefirelegacy.org by Dallas Henslee on 06/05/20

Be Set On Fire for God's Kingdom

"For this reason I remind you to fan into flame the gift of God, which is in you through the laying on of my hands, for God gave us a spirit not of fear but of power and love and self-control." (2 Timothy 1:6-7, ESV)

We live in the Colorado mountains at 8000 feet. One winter we had electric heat and a wood burning stove. Since the electricity costs money, we attempted to use the wood stove as much as possible to heat the house. I'd spend time each day lighting the fire in the stove. Each time, I would think about the statement from Paul, "...fan into flame the gift of God, which is in you...." (2 Timothy 1:6, ESV)

In order for the fire to be beneficial in the early stages, we need flames. It is the flames that ignite the wood that produces the heat which is what we need. Often there are embers that glow which later in the fire stage do produce good heat, but early on are not sufficient. If I walk away with just a few embers glowing, it won't be long before there is no fire at all. That can make for a cold night.

Fanning the embers into flame takes a few things. We need a flame source, such as a lighter. Then we need a starter material that will burn easily, such as paper, which will then get the larger pieces of wood burning. We also need an air source and adequate space for the flame because if we stack the paper and wood too tightly, it won't burn. Put all this together and we can have a fire that burns and produces the needed heat.

Our Life is to Be a Burning Fire for the World

In our life, we need to follow Paul's instruction to fan into flame the gifts that God has placed in our life. We need to be a light and heat source to the dark, cold world around us.

What gifts do you have that the world needs? Are you good at caring for people? Do you have the ability to encourage? Maybe you have a passion to serve others.

You may be an incredible businessperson who can make lots of money for the Kingdom of God. There is a need for individuals to financially support those who are called to go.

Whatever your gifts and passions, use them to minister to others. The world needs God's love to be displayed in a wide array of manners.

What Do We Need to Burn?

As with a physical fire, we need a few things in our life to be set ablaze for God's Kingdom. We need the Word of God (the Bible), the Holy Spirit, and enough space in our life to burn.

Our starter material is the Word of God

Read the Bible. Make time to read it every day. Read all of scripture, not just the easy stories. Study the Word with purpose and understanding. It is not enough to just touch the surface or read a little here and there. We need to dig deep into the Word. We need enough of Scripture each day to ignite our life so that we will burn with heat to benefit the world around us.

A friend recently completed reading the entire Bible in a year for the first time in his life. He was so excited about the connections that he was seeing between the different books of the Bible. As he began to read through a second time, he said that it was so much more meaningful because of the understanding that he had gained from those passages that he hadn't read before.

I like to read different translations of the Bible. It gets me thinking differently than how I've always seen or heard the passages. Having a slightly different wording or a significantly different twist via a paraphrase can cause me to think about the passage more deeply.

The Bible is God's Word. It is not just a book of stories. It is alive and has real meaning for our lives. No matter how many times I read through all of it, there is so much more that I discover each time.

Our ignition source is the Holy Spirit

What is going to ignite the flame in us? We need the Holy Spirit to open our eyes to see and ears to hear as we read Scripture.

It is through the Holy Spirit that we are able to have understanding and to apply the Word to us and to others.

In Acts 2, God describes the Holy Spirit as tongues of fire that came to rest upon the disciples. Jesus promised to send a Counselor, One who guides and teaches (John 16:7). And He did send the Holy Spirit.

We need to be willing to listen to the Holy Spirit's guidance. In our daily lives, we need to hear those prompts to help others. It may be something seemingly insignificant to us, but to the other person it may be just what they needed to handle their situation. So much of what we do can have an impact far greater than we'll ever know when we are obedient to the Holy Spirit.

We need space in our life

Finally, we need to have the space around us to allow the fire to burn. We need to reduce our schedules. We need to slow down and have time with the Father in worship. We need to have time to meditate on Scripture. We need to take time to have conversations with God – prayer is not just us talking, it is also us listening.

I'm one who has a strong tendency to overcommit and to remain very busy, all the time, continually, without stopping. The Lord has been working very hard on me the past couple years to learn how to slow down and make the space needed in my life. There have been days that I've felt like I've been pulled from the game and put on the bench. This has been necessary for me to learn to make the space needed for the Lord to burn in me.

I've had to learn about and apply the Sabbath to my life. It's not just one of the Ten Commandments. It is a vital practice for our physical and spiritual health. Jesus said, "The Sabbath was made for man, not man for the Sabbath" (Mark 2:27, ESV). We need the Sabbath.

In addition to practicing a Sabbath rest, we need to open up the remainder of our week for the Lord to have space to work through us. If we are running late all the time, when do we have the ability to pause and help someone on the way? If our schedule is too full, how can we meet with another for encouragement? If we don't have time to breathe, how can we "Be still, and know that I am God...." (Psalms 46:10, ESV)?

Fan Your Life into Flames

How about you? Are you burning with the gift of God which is in you?

We need to get into the Word of God with the Holy Spirit so that God's gift inside of us will burn with flames to benefit the world around us. We need to make the space needed in our lives for the Holy Spirit to work through us. Gather the needed materials, do the prep work, and be the light and heat that is needed in the world around you.

Originally posted on www.bluefirelegacy.org by Mark Henslee on 08/31/18

3

Obedience and Faith

Living Right-Side Up in an Upside-Down World

"For as the heavens are higher than the earth, so are my ways higher than your ways and my thoughts than your thoughts." (Isaiah 55:9, ESV)

I've been told that I'm not normal. And it's true. For as long as I can remember, I haven't seen things in the manner that most people view them. In the last few years, my perspective on things has gone even further out of line, from the "normal" world.

It can be a difficult life when you are misunderstood. A few years ago, I started to figure out why I view things so differently. I'm upside down from the world's views.

Buying an RV

God has us do things differently on a regular basis. Take for example, our recent negotiation to purchase a 5th wheel travel trailer for the ministry.

Dallas was scrolling through her Facebook page and came across a 5th wheel RV for sale. The asking price was $12,500 which was less than the $12,800 the ministry had in its RV fund. After looking at the pictures, Dallas messaged the seller, to arrange a time to look at the trailer. I started to look at what this model was selling for, and all of the listings were from $18,000 to $24,000. Now, I was wondering, "What was wrong with this one?"

The trailer is 13 years old so there are a few things that need attention, but it fits the main criteria that we need for counseling and ministering on the road. Both of us had a peace from the Lord to proceed with the purchase.

When I started to talk about the price, confirming that he was asking $12,500, he got a bit uncomfortable. He had realized the asking price was too low and removed the original post, relisting the trailer for $15,000.

We only had $12,800 in the RV fund for a purchase. I told him how much we had and that we were buying it for a ministry. I had previously asked if he would be willing to deliver it to our house, because we don't have a tow vehicle, and he had agreed. Since he was delivering it, he asked if we could pay $13,000. I thought we could take $200 from the general fund and make that happen. We agreed to a sale price of $13,000 upon receiving approval from our Board.

Abnormal Negotiations

On the drive home, Dallas said, "What if we paid him $13,500?" This isn't how most purchase negotiations work. Generally, the buyer tries to get the lowest price and pays what is agreed upon, not more. However, I felt that this was from the Lord and would bring Him great honor as a testimony to His great provision, not just for us, but also for the seller. So, we presented the idea to the Board for their input and approval. By the end of the evening, we had unanimous approval from the Board, and I messaged the seller that we would pay him $13,500 for the trailer.

The next day, we spoke, and he gave me his bank information, so that I could transfer the money. He was to come by our house after work and bring the title. Another unusual thing that I did was to move all of the funds without seeing the title. Normally, you would do that simultaneously. Humanly, I questioned what I was doing, but felt that the Lord was in it, so we would be okay. The seller did show up that evening with a clear title in hand. He also came through with delivering the trailer to our house later that week, a day earlier than expected.

This is not a normal way of doing things! But it is God's way of doing things, and He will be glorified.

Throughout the entire process, we shared about the Lord and how good He is to us. The seller was open to hear and even asked about our church. We are praying that he and his young family will come to know the Lord personally.

Viewing Things From a Different Perspective

When we start to look at the world from God's perspective, we see things differently. God's Kingdom is right-side up, which means our world is upside-down. We have been trained to look at things from the upside-down view for so long that we think it is right-side up, but it's not. We need to reorient to God's ways.

Too many of us try to make God fit into our way of viewing things. We miss so much, when we fail to see as He sees. We need His perspective.

We generally look at things the way we have been taught by those around us. We see ourselves as insignificant or unworthy. God sees us as His beloved children.

As we transition to being right-side up, it can be rather disorienting. If you flip back and forth continually, it can be really disorienting. For those who have taken a flight in an acrobatic airplane with a skilled pilot, they know just how disorienting, and possibly nauseating, it can be to flip around, rolling and tossing. Some get a thrill, others just want to be back on solid ground.

Personally, I love flying in a small airplane, in smooth air, but I don't like rolls and flips. As I'm learning to walk in God's ways, I find it best to not be flipping back to the old ways of thinking and acting.

Difficult Conversations

As we make the shift to God's view, we can become disoriented because it feels so different, and sometimes even wrong. We may even be wishing to just go back to the "solid ground" of our past ways. Unfortunately, that solid ground is really shaky, like shifting sand.

Our family and friends will very likely look at us with concern. These can be difficult conversations to have. I know, I've had many of them.

Everything that they are saying makes complete sense, and yet I'm disagreeing with the conclusion. There have been several occasions where I've been thinking to myself, "If I was in their place, I'd be saying the exact same things. Maybe I've completely lost my mind."

And yet, I can still say very clearly, with great confidence, that we need to do things the way God says, not how it makes sense to us.

These conversations have led to more than one occasion to practice forgiveness on both sides. I hope that I'm getting better at having these difficult conversations with an attitude of love, though I know I still have room for improvement.

His Ways are Better

The more I walk in His uprightness and viewpoint, the more comfortable I am becoming with doing things differently, than I always thought. I have grown in my faith and understanding of who I am in Christ. There is great security in knowing that I'm a beloved child of God. There is also freedom to make mistakes.

> *"For my thoughts are not your thoughts,*
> *neither are your ways my ways, declares*
> *the Lord.*
> *For as the heavens are higher than the earth,*
> *so are my ways higher than your ways*
> *and my thoughts than your thoughts."*
> *(Isaiah 55:8-9, ESV)*

Our time here on earth is a short part of our eternal life. We need to start living from God's eternal Kingdom perspective.

How are you viewing the things of life? Are you willing to go through the uncomfortable, in order to align with God's right-side up Kingdom?

Originally posted on www.bluefirelegacy.org by Mark Henslee on 08/20/21

From Selfish to Sacrificial Living

"...become all things to all people, that by all means I might save some." (1 Corinthians 9:22b, ESV)

I'm generally a selfish person, have been all of my life. When I was a young kid, I would throw temper tantrums when I didn't get what I wanted. It didn't matter if it was a particular food (I was one of those picky eaters), or the ability to play with what I wanted, or just to be alone (I'm a natural introvert). I could throw the biggest, ugliest tantrums any little kid has pulled off before. My mom was a saint for having to deal with me, and she did it with such grace and love.

As an adult, my tantrums look different, but are still there. They are generally more internal than external now. Over the years, I've shared about some of my "conversations" with God where things were not as I expected or wanted. Much like my mom, He listens and continues to love me, even in my ugliness.

Sick to Death

Recently, I battled through a bout of the virus that has plagued the world the last couple of years. I ran a fever for 14 days, my body did things that are not normal or right, I couldn't think straight, reading was impossible, my brain and body did not work properly, and generally, I felt horrible.

Unfortunately, Dallas was also sick, so we pretty much had to fend for ourselves. Normally, we take care of each other when one is ill. Those two weeks were absolutely miserable. Fortunately, our church family brought food and drinks, and helped as best they could.

I don't do sick well. When I don't feel good, I tend to become very self-focused and needy. This illness took that to another level. In the midst of the battle, I told the Lord that was enough, either take me home or heal me. I wasn't worried about Dallas or my kids or anyone else. I just wanted the suffering to end. In effect, I was throwing another tantrum.

Out of that time of suffering, I've come to a new understanding of what it means to live life sacrificially. In Philippians 1:21, Paul says, "For me to live is Christ, and to die is gain." I'm still learning what he meant when he wrote this. To live life for Christ is not a natural outflow from my human nature. However, we are called to live in the supernatural, therefore we need to learn to live as a living sacrifice.

No Fear of Death

We are assured of death in this life. It's something that is guaranteed for all of us. However, there is a second death that we can avoid. The only way to have eternal life is through Christ Jesus. There are a lot of good sounding theologies that provide alternative paths, but only *one* is the way. Even though death is certain, we don't need to fear it, if we are in a right relationship with God.

I don't have any fear of death. In fact, the thought of eternity with my Lord is very appealing. I don't look forward to the process of dying, but the afterlife is exciting to think about. This is the part that Paul is talking about when he said, "to die is gain". The assurance of salvation and eternity is a great blessing.

It's the living part of life that I sometimes struggle to handle well.

Hardship is Going to Happen

Nowhere in Scripture do I find a promise of an easy life after we receive Christ as our Savior. In fact, I see multiple passages that tell us to expect trials, tribulations, and hardship. See James 1:2-4 and Romans 5:3-5 for two examples. We are to face these hardships in the Lord's strength, and grow through them. They should build our endurance and character.

Paul talked about his thorn in the flesh that he struggled with for years (see 2 Corinthians 12:7-9). If the apostle who wrote a large chunk of the New Testament wasn't exempt from hardship, why would we expect to be?

Too often, we just want to give up in the midst of our trials. I know I did when I was sick. But the reality is that we shouldn't be living for ourselves. Therefore, we need to change our focus from us to the Lord and those around us.

To Live is Christ

Paul surrendered his life, including his rights, to live as the Lord directed. This is not an easy thing to do. It requires great sacrifice of self. He was willing to "become all things to all people, that by all means I might save some." (1 Corinthians 9:22b, ESV) That's true selfless living. That is to live completely in Christ.

I don't know about you, but I'm still working on getting to a fully surrendered life. I'm learning and growing. Some days, I do better than others. I've made strides in the process, and yet, there is more to change.

My life objective for many years has been to be Christ-like. I had no idea what I was committing to when I made that decision. The hardships of the past years have seemed insurmountable in the moment, and yet, I can look back and see all the good that has come from those hard times. Hard does not equal bad. In fact, many of the best things come through hardship.

For me, as a husband, part of living a sacrificial life is to love my wife as Christ loved the Church. The instructions found in Ephesians 5:25-33 are often overlooked in our attempts to be the head of the household. Jesus often demonstrated leadership by serving those he led. We need to be doing the same.

Committed to a Sacrificial Life

I am committed again to live life completely surrendered to the Lord. For me to live is to put others before myself, to do things that I don't want to do because the Lord tells me to do it, to accept that it's not about me. My life is the Lord's, not my own.

I know I will fall short at times but that doesn't mean I'm not going to strive for the goal. How about you? Are you willing to put yourself aside and live surrendered? I encourage you to join me in the journey. It's hard, but oh so good.

Originally posted on www.bluefirelegacy.org by Mark Henslee on 11/19/21

Our Opinions Provide Comfort in the Absence of God's Perspective

"Many are the plans in the mind of a man, but it is the purpose of the Lord that will stand."

(Proverbs 19:21, ESV)

We all have opinions on things. I have lots of opinions. Some of them are probably worth something, and others are mere thoughts without much merit. Yet, we live the majority of our life based on our opinions of how things should, or should not, be done. What is right and wrong. How we think things should be.

When we were in the process of starting the ministry back in 2015, I had things mapped out and *lots* of ideas of how it was going to work. I also had a few strong opinions. We would have an RV that allowed us to travel to the clients. The building at Legacy Heights would be built relatively soon providing a place for us to office and for ministers to retreat. The buyer of my CPA firm would be successful, and we could live on the residual payments. It was going to be good.

By August of 2016 when we sold our house, we were faced with where to live. Instead of having an RV as I had expected, we had nowhere to go. I would tell people that God would take care of us. A relative point blank said, "Seriously, where are you going to live?" For some reason, they didn't think homelessness was a good answer.

There were people who would send us links for various RVs. Many of these qualified as campers, and others simply looked unlivable, let alone *drivable* across the country. This was also during the time that tiny houses were being promoted, and we had plenty of people encouraging us to get a tiny house to put on Legacy Heights. Good, well-meaning people that love us. Yet, their ideas were not in line with the vision we believe God gave for the ministry.

I Had Plans

I used to have a five year plan and a ten year plan along with short-term plans for what I wanted to accomplish in life. My plans were generally built around what I wanted or thought would be good.

Then one day God got my attention. He asked if I was willing to give Him my plans and, in exchange, live completely dependent upon Him. That was not an easy decision to make. It was rather painful at the time and even continues to be difficult as we walk out the process of life in His ways.

Today, instead of a five or ten year plan, I normally have a general idea about what life *may* look like in the next one to three months. Sometimes, we get to plan an activity or trip further out but not often. It's not a normal American lifestyle, but the Lord has proven to be amazing as we journey with Him.

Our Thoughts Versus His Thoughts

It is important to use our brains and reason. After all, God did create us with a mind to think and process information. However, we don't want to get stuck in our limited understanding and reason. We don't want to miss God when He doesn't make sense to us.

Isaiah 55:8, ESV says, "For my thoughts are not your thoughts, neither are your ways my ways, declares the Lord." We often struggle with understanding God's thoughts and ways. They are so different from ours, and so much better. The next verse tells us why. "For as the heavens are higher than the earth, so are my ways higher than your ways and my thoughts than your thoughts."

Sometimes what we think of a situation is irrelevant. I'm yet to have the President of the United States call me up for my opinion on anything. Believe me, I have opinions that he needs to hear, but he still hasn't asked me for them. Why not? Because I'm not in a position of trust, never mind that he doesn't even know my name.

I also don't necessarily have all of the information to be able to rightly assess the situation. God sees everything, yet I see very little. My perspective is very limited along with my knowledge and understanding. I like to think that I know it all, but really, I don't (shh, don't tell my kids).

Hearing Clearly

When God speaks, we have a tendency to hear what we want to hear. We may embellish that dream we had, or interpret the word received from the limited perspective we see. Our desires or fears can get in the way of hearing clearly everything that He is saying.

Confirmation with other people can be very beneficial. Proverbs repeatedly tells us to seek wise counsel (Proverbs 11:14, 12:15, 15:22, 19:20 and 24:6). Unfortunately, sometimes that Godly man or woman that we look up to is giving their opinion and not God's. It's common for even our trusted advisors to have limited perspective that distorts their input. We need to be careful with how much trust we put in the words of another person.

Ultimately, it is God's opinion and Word that matters. What we think or want is irrelevant in our journey as Christ followers. We have to be willing to sacrifice our everything to be successful in taking up our cross and following Him.

Is God asking you to trade your plans for a life fully dependent upon Him? Five and a half years into my journey of laying down my plans, I can say, "It's an adventure that I don't want to ever miss out on."

Originally posted on www.bluefirelegacy.org by Mark Henslee on 03/19/21

We Bring the Sacrifice of Praise, Service and Worship

"Through him then let us continually offer up a sacrifice of praise to God, that is, the fruit of lips that acknowledge his name." (Hebrews 13:15, ESV)

We held our third night of collective community worship events last night. As the musicians prepared and rehearsed, we looked a little at what worship is and what it is not. I shared a devotional with them which included an excerpt from *How To Worship A King* by Zach Neese found on pp. 13-14. The author shares a poignant lesson from God regarding worship and how he was forever changed because of this encounter.

In all candor, this worship event was the most difficult to plan and execute to date. While we have met challenges such as losing a musician or last-minute venue changes in prior events, this time, we were assaulted for a lengthy period of time leading up to being together in corporate worship.

There was the initial struggle of finding enough musicians. Then, throughout the week before, we started having to work through losing an instrumentalist (with the potential of losing a second from our already skeleton-like band), a vocalist, and a worship flagger due to various complications. We also experienced additional emotional strain from extended family circumstances. For the second time, there was inclement weather forecasted for the day we had scheduled to hold the event outdoors. In addition to all the above, I could hardly get out of bed due to physical fatigue, nausea, and a wicked headache.

Overcoming Problems with Sacrifice

This posed a pretty big problem since I typically lead the group. Mark prayed over me before heading to church to help with the praise team, Sunday School, and morning service. I was so physically depleted, he was running alternative scenarios through his mind, although he admitted none of them were very good. He decided that regardless of who did or didn't make it, there would be worship that evening.

Recognizing this was a spiritual attack by the enemy, I continued to get up in short spurts to work towards getting ready. I probably topped out at 20-30 minutes before going back to bed at each attempt.

As I was in bed, the Lord and I were talking about what was going on. Through past experiences, Mark and I have learned that resistance is almost always an indication that God has something big and awesome in store. So, we tend to have some level of excitement mixed in with the need to walk through the difficult circumstances.

I managed to keep some saltine crackers and ginger ale down by 2:00 that afternoon. And, as I got up and around, it was easier to get dressed and load up the last few items of equipment needed for the evening.

Laying Our Isaac Down

At the event, I read Hebrews 13:15, ESV. *"Through Him"*....there was no other way I was able to be present and lead. I like the ESV and NLT versions of this verse so I've included both for your reference.

"Through him then let us continually offer up a sacrifice of praise to God, that is, the fruit of lips that acknowledge his name." (Hebrews 13:15, ESV)

"Therefore, let us offer through Jesus a continual sacrifice of praise to God, proclaiming our allegiance to his name." (Hebrews 13:15, NLT)

I shared that offering a sacrifice of praise can come in a variety of ways:

- Worshiping when you can hardly lift your head and get out of bed (check)
- Worshiping in the midst of grief in various contexts (check)
- Worshiping when it's inconvenient in your schedule or when you're tired
- Worshiping when you know it will impact your body negatively [i.e. blisters, aches and pains from standing so long, waving a flag, or from the weight of holding an instrument] (check)

- Worshiping even when it's a style you don't typically enjoy
- Worshiping through submitting to a fast prescribed by the Lord (partial check--ginger ale and crackers aren't very filling)
- Worshiping through the act of service in the form of manual labor; set up and tear down require effort
- Worshiping through (I'm sure you can think of something else that applies to you that could go on this list.)

See, when we remember that praise and worship isn't for us, it's easier to place our "Isaac" on the altar. Worship was designed by God for His pleasure. It is our privilege to minister to Him through devotion, music, dance, flags, etc.

Make A Joyful Noise

He can even take pleasure in something we would label a "train wreck" if our hearts are in the right place. Worship isn't performance. Worship is coming before Him and being in His Presence. It is all about Him. He can take pleasure in a joyful noise when our hearts are submitted to Him. Which is a good thing, since we had one of those train wreck (aka joyful noise) moments in the midst of the songs last night.

"Make a joyful noise unto the Lord, all the earth: make a loud noise, and rejoice, and sing praise." (Psalms 98:4, ESV)

"Make a joyful noise to the Lord, all the earth! Serve the Lord with gladness! Come into his presence with singing! Know that the Lord, he is God!   It is he who made us, and we are his; we are his people, and the sheep of his pasture. Enter his gates with thanksgiving, and his courts with praise! Give thanks to him; bless his name! For the Lord is good; his steadfast love endures forever, and his faithfulness to all generations." (Psalms 100:1-5, ESV)

Mark said you'd never know I had been so sick and feeble earlier in the day based on what happened at the worship night. We did excerpts from 42 songs as we worshiped through the decades for over 90 minutes. I give all the credit to the Lord for giving me strength, energy, endurance, and a strong voice; none of which should have been possible physically speaking.

The hardest event to date was also the most powerful and intimate in coming before the Lord. I believe He was pleased with the offering of our praise and worship. You were born to worship; even when it requires bringing your sacrifice of praise!

Originally posted on www.bluefirelegacy.org by Dallas Henslee on 06/04/21

Plucking Sentimental Heart Strings to Resolve Dissonant Chords

"Draw near to God, and he will draw near to you. Cleanse your hands, you sinners, and purify your hearts, you double-minded." (James 4:8, ESV)

Dissonant Disagreement

When you hear a dissonant chord, typically something inside you longs for it to be resolved. It creates a tension that begs to be released. Whether you experience this only on an audible level or you understand it from the theory construct, this type of chord often leads to another.

Another field which employs a similar term is psychology. In this field, you often hear of cognitive dissonance meaning there are competing thoughts. Again, wrestling through the different perspectives competing to come out on top indicates the need for one thought to come under submission to the other. Resolution; one is looking to arrive at resolution or at least a place of acceptable conclusion.

What happens when God asks you to do something you really don't want to do? Dissonance. Your desires (will) are competing with God's.

I found myself in this uncomfortable space when my love of creating music on my piano and competing thoughts collided as God transitioned us from a life of relative ease and financial security into full-time ministry and founding Blue Fire Legacy.

Part of that transition required us to sell our home. At the time, we thought He was asking us to move into an RV as our full-time dwelling, so we were selling and giving away furniture. We had planned to keep a few pieces, primarily those handed down in the family and select other pieces, but largely, we had decided that we were to downsize drastically.

Drastically Downsizing

One of my friends was aware of a missionary family that was returning to the United States that needed to furnish a home. "Do you have anything they might want?" she asked. I put together an extensive list of items for them to look through, and we arranged a time for them to come pick up the items they desired.

After we made the arrangements for a day and time, I felt God asking, "What about the piano? Would you give them your piano?" Those two questions not only created cognitive dissonance, but made my heart feel as if someone had struck a harsh chord that had no resolution.

"Oh, Lord, not the piano. Please, not the piano." This was not just any piano. It was the piano I learned to play on from my childhood. It was often a place of comfort and solace or a meeting place with God in an intimate way. Immediate willingness and obedience was not present. I was going to have to fight through this direct request.

On one hand, it was irreplaceable because of its sentimental value. On the other hand, I'd wanted to upgrade pianos for a while. It wouldn't be able to go with us in the RV, but we could store it. However, in my heart, I knew that storing it indefinitely was bad for the instrument itself and could even mean its complete demise in the dry Colorado climate.

Out the Door

Finally, I said, "If they specifically ask about the piano, Lord." Of course, I was hoping they wouldn't ask, and I wasn't willing to go out of my way to offer it.

The missionaries came to pick up the furniture that we had agreed to give them. I was about to close the door behind him as he walked out. He turned around and asked, "What about the piano? My wife hasn't had a piano to play in years, and I know she would really like to have one."

I heard myself say, "The Lord and I have been talking about that. I'll get back to you closer to time for us to move out of the house."

They became the proud owners of that well-loved, used, Story and Clark piano, but I wasn't home when they came to load it up. Amazingly, we received word that God had it arrive in another city about an hour north of us *in tune* after leaving my house greatly in need of a tuning appointment.

My heart strings were plucked. Sometimes I still ache to have a piano to sit down and play, but the resolution, relief, and transition to a more pleasant place come with knowing that God used me to provide for another. I have the ability to rejoice not only in my obedience, but in the joy it gave her.

Resolving Dissonance

Do you have times when what you want to do and what God says is acceptable don't play nice together or strike a pleasing harmony? It may be that you need to take stock of what's in your life and decide if you will allow the Lord to reign, or if you are going to reserve just that one little thing; that thought, behavior, dream, relationship, possession, position, income…. Is Jesus at the door asking if you will surrender something you are emotionally attached to? If He is, it's time to give it to Him. Your obedience and surrender will bring Him great joy, and you will be blessed through your act of obedience.

Originally posted on www.bluefirelegacy.org by Dallas Henslee on 11/23/18

The Incredible Power of Music in Our Lives

"Let the word of Christ dwell in you richly, teaching and admonishing one another in all wisdom, singing psalms and hymns and spiritual songs, with thankfulness in your hearts to God." (Colossians 3:16, ESV)

In sixth grade, I was in the band room, after jazz band practice, on what was otherwise a normal Thursday. Kids were talking about popular songs of the day, and I felt weird that I didn't really know them. Wanting to fit in, I was thinking that I needed to start listening to the radio stations that they listened to and learn the music.

Right there, as if a person had walked up to me, I felt the Lord ask a very clear question. "Are you willing to not listen to secular music for the rest of your life?" There wasn't a command in the question. It was as if I could say, "yes" or "no", and He would continue to love and accept me either way.

As I thought about the question, my hesitation was that I wouldn't fit in with the other kids. I don't remember expressing that thought, but He clearly told me that would be a sacrifice, if I chose to make the commitment.

The second, and probably larger, concern I had was that I would not be able to enjoy music anymore. You see, what I knew of Christian music at the time wasn't really my style. I enjoy a very large variety of styles of music, including jazz and classical, but my "go to" is rock. My mom's Christian radio station was okay, but it was mellow and definitely not rock.

Without much more thought, I said, "Yes, I'll commit to that." The conversation with the other kids continued, but I just listened, mostly wondering what I had committed myself to for life. I don't think that all secular music is wrong or that God asks this of all believers. I need to be obedient to what He asks of me.

Music is Universal

Music transcends language, race, and culture. There is an exceedingly wide variety of styles, rhythms and general "feels" to music around the globe, but all people seemingly have an internal ability to relate to music. I've heard many songs sung with the same tune in multiple languages. It's as if God created music to be a part of the internal being of all people.

Music touches our emotions. It can be calming, encouraging, and even enraging. What we are feeling seems to be intensified when expressed through music.

Music has been used to express rebellion. Each generation seems to use music as a means of separating and differentiating themselves from their parents. And yet, we also use music to bring people together.

Music and the Brain

We learn better when the concept is put to music. How many of us learned our ABC's by singing the song? I remember when my kids were at a charter school, they had a song for the presidents, the states, and several other lists of things. It was a tool used by the teachers to get the kids to memorize a vast amount of information more easily.

Music clearly has a connection to how our brains process information and learn. It's believed that kids that play an instrument do better in school and later in life. I'm no expert, but apparently playing music, even simple instruments, helps with brain development.

Playing music in the background will somehow be absorbed into our minds. We don't have to be purposefully listening to the words, and yet, somehow, we know them. When we sing along to the songs, we are encoding those words and thoughts deep inside of us.

Deep in Memory

If you put on a Petra song from the 1980s, even if I haven't heard that song in years, I will most likely be able to sing along with the majority of the words. These days, I struggle to remember things I heard just this week. Tell me your name, and I may not remember it in five minutes. How can I remember words to a song I haven't heard in years? There is a strong imprinting on our memories when we listen to music, especially over and over again. I remember those Petra songs, because I listened to the albums and sang the songs.

Most people, who have enjoyed music and listened to it for years, have similar abilities to recall tunes and lyrics. Even people who don't regularly listen to music can relatively quickly identify the theme song of different TV shows, movies, or talk radio programs. The spoken word has less impact on our memories compared to music.

When you look at the hymns across the ages, you will see songwriters that put theology to music. They even put a few to bar tunes. How scandalous! Apparently, they knew that we don't remember much that the preacher says, but at least they could get us to learn through the songs being sung. Some ministers even plan the church service, so that the songs coincide with the sermon message, aiding the congregants to take something into their week.

Over the Years

It's been a long time since I made that commitment back in sixth grade. I've missed out on being able to participate in many conversations about this song or that band. But then, I seem to have missed many of the hip and stylish trends over the years.

In the couple years that I was angry at God and not in church, I even tried to listen to the popular radio stations, but I couldn't. When I was mad at God and didn't want Him speaking to me, I couldn't break the commitment made. It wasn't a conscious decision about keeping it. Trying to listen to secular music just grated on my soul. I ended up creating a couple of instrumental-only stations on my streaming service.

By the way, I got to enjoy rock as a teenager, listening to screaming guitars and heavy drums, all with Christian lyrics. When I go back and look at the lyrics of the songs, there was some good theology that I didn't even realize was there at the time. Today, I still enjoy the rock beat and feel. There's not much that is more fun for me than playing bass with a drummer beating away, and an electric guitarist making their guitar scream, while singing praises to my Lord.

I believe the Lord asked me to make that commitment years ago, because He wanted the best for me. At the time, I thought it was a sacrifice. Now, I'm glad I did it. I've gotten to enjoy some great music over the years, and my mind has absorbed a lot of good lessons.

What about you? What are you absorbing in your soul through the music you listen to and sing?

Originally posted on www.bluefirelegacy.org by Mark Henslee on 06/18/21

Is It Okay to Wrestle with God?

"Fear not, for I am with you; be not dismayed, for I am your God; I will strengthen you, I will help you, I will uphold you with my righteous right hand." (Isaiah 41:10, ESV)

As a young child, I was an expert in throwing temper tantrums. My mom should have been sainted for having to handle me in those years. I could be incredibly difficult. Yelling, screaming, physically destructive, and emotionally hurtful to those around me.

Looking back, I don't think that I had an ability to properly express my feelings, so I just threw a tantrum. Unlike our earthly parents, God knows exactly how we feel whether we express it or not.

There are times in life when things aren't going the way we think they should. We know that God is there and working in our life. We may even be in a place to worship Him and pray, but there is a disconnect. We have a hurt or struggle with Him that we're not even sure how to identify, let alone how to express. What do we do then?

We know that God is a Good Father, that He is holy and worthy of our worship and honor. We generally approach Him with the respect that He deserves. And then there are those times when we just want to scream at Him. Is this allowed? Will He strike us with lightning if we let loose?

To Scream or Be Silent?

God is able to smite us, but He doesn't. He is big enough to handle our tantrums. I think He even prefers that we scream at Him instead of being silent and ignoring Him.

When my kids were young, we would have *those* days. I remember having to wrap my arms and legs around them as they kicked and screamed. Holding them with all the love that I had until they would settle down. It may have seemed like I was being mean, but I was actually protecting them from hurting themself or others.

This may sound weird, but now that my kids are adults, I would rather they yell and scream than to be silent and avoid me. Because I value our relationship, I still want to be engaged with them even in the hard times. God also wants us to interact with Him, even when we are struggling with things in our life or with Him.

Biblical Examples

Jacob wrestled with God (or an angel, it's unclear) through the night (Genesis 32:22-32). Job wrestled with God but kept his integrity (Book of Job). Jesus wrestled in the Garden of Gethsemane (Matthew 26:39-42).

Each example is different, but they all have some things in common. The men came into conflict with the Almighty God.

They did not curse God, but they did question Him. Each was willing to submit to God's plan after the time of wrestling. In the end, each was blessed by God. When we wrestle with God, we will be changed by the experience.

Free Will

Do you ever wonder why God, in His infinite wisdom and knowledge, would give us free-will? Think about it. He knew that we would goof things up. He knew that we wouldn't get it right every time. Yet, He still gives us the freedom to choose.

I know that I like to have control in my life, so it's nice to have free-will for myself. Sometimes, I like to have control in the lives of others around me, even though in reality I have very little, if any, ability to control another.

I think that God gave us free-will because He wants to walk in relationship with us. If He just dictated everything or we didn't have the ability to choose, that wouldn't be much of a relationship. Respect given freely is better than given out of fear. The love that I receive from my wife and kids is so much sweeter knowing that they have made the choice to love me (even with all my faults). God enjoys our praise, love, and adoration more when given out of our choosing than if we give out of fear or obligation.

Our Will

In most situations that we claim to be wrestling with God, the reality is that we are wrestling with our own will. As followers of Christ, we are new creations with old habits and thought patterns. We struggle with our fallen human nature as we strive to be Christ-like. Paul describes this battle in Romans 7:15, ESV. "For I do not understand my own actions. For I do not do what I want, but I do the very thing I hate."

"For those who live according to the flesh set their minds on the things of the flesh, but those who live according to the Spirit set their minds on the things of the Spirit. For to set the mind on the flesh is death, but to set the mind on the Spirit is life and peace." (Romans 8:5-6, ESV)

We must change the focus of our thoughts. It is easy to think according to the flesh but that will lead to death. We must crucify our own will and way of thinking and put on the mind of Christ (1 Corinthians 2:16). It is only through Christ that we will be able to live in peace.

Is It Okay?

Is it okay to wrestle with God? I think so. In my hurt, anger, disappointment, frustration, or whatever other time that I've yelled and screamed at God, He has always responded with love beyond measure. I have been changed through my times of wrestling with Him. And ultimately, as I become more like Christ, He blesses me beyond anything that I could ever deserve.

Originally posted on www.bluefirelegacy.org by Mark Henslee on 04/26/19

Waving the Flag of Conditional Surrender

"Then he arose and went after Elijah and assisted him."

(1 Kings 19:21b, ESV)

Our small groups at church are using a series which depicts Jesus' life. One of the episodes focuses on the moment Simon Peter chose to follow the Lord. There are many stories like this in the Bible. Let me remind you of just a couple; one in the Old Testament and one in the New.

There is the story of Elijah and Elisha in 1 Kings. When Elisha felt compelled to follow the call of ministry and assist Elijah, he communicated personal devotion and surrender by giving up his livelihood and saying goodbye to his family (1 Kings 19:19-21).

In the same New Testament passage that tells us about Simon Peter and Andrew abandoning their nets to follow Jesus, we also see James and John. They were with their father, Zebedee, in the boat tending to the family business, when Jesus called them. They also left their nets behind without reservation. In fact, the Bible says, "Immediately, they left their boat and their father and followed him." (Matthew 4:22, ESV)

Real People with Real Decisions

Real people, just like you and me, making a life altering decision. Jesus was in their midst and they were convicted. We have their testimonies as recorded in the Bible, in addition to the presence of the Holy Spirit; and yet, sadly, many today hear and heed the voice of reservation over the call of the Savior.

When we look at heroes of the faith, we often admire their ability to trust God completely; their ability to be fully submitted to His sovereignty. Then, in our mind, there is a weird twist that happens as we ponder our own decision to submit. It often sounds like, "I could never do *that*!"

Unfortunately, many Christians find themselves growing stale in their faith because they've agreed to lies just like that one. The temptation comes in the form of a perceived life of ease and desires met for the remainder of one's lifetime. This can lead one to begin to live a lifestyle of conditional submission without even realizing it. Conditional submission or surrender is revealed by our thoughts or actions which establish, "I'll do what God asks if…."

- If it's easy.
- If it's what I want.
- If it meets all my expectations.
- If (fill in the blank with your personal condition).

I hope you bristle somewhat at each of those statements. See, the thing is, "conditional" and "surrender" simply cannot co-exist in a Christ-centered life. Either you limit God, and therefore, say, "No" in some manner, or you fully submit and surrender.

Step into His Way

The latter goes completely against Western culture which expects you to be in charge of your own life and destiny. God's not bound to culture. In fact, Mark and I often talk about God turning us right-side up in an upside-down world and tease each other about Him shaking up our snow globe when major plans change. This has become our norm. We don't know how to live differently anymore. It makes small talk at gatherings a little more difficult, though, because we struggle to find commonality for chit chat conversations.

This dynamic was highlighted several years ago when we were invited to visit a small community group and share about Blue Fire Legacy. The men and women split into smaller groups for eating and visiting with each other. The women were talking about pop culture and current television programming. I was completely lost. It was uncomfortable to have nothing to offer or even be able to join in as an included fringe participant. When I checked in with Mark later in the evening about the men's conversation for this portion of the evening, he said that he was similarly uncomfortable even though the subject matter discussed by the men was different than the ladies.

It's not that we're dull. It's just that we tend to have a lot of God stories, and not everyone wants to hear those. Well, that, and people have a hard time understanding exactly what we do so even those basic conversations can quickly become a little awkward.

Burn the Ships & Cut the Ties

For the past decade, complete surrender for us has looked like becoming completely dependent on the Lord's financial provision; closing a private counseling practice, transitioning a thriving accounting practice to a buyer that closed it within a year and a half of purchase, selling the house we raised our 3 children in, paying off all our debt, being homeless for just over a year, re-entering ministry by founding Blue Fire Legacy making that our full-time emphasis, establishing community in a small town in Colorado where we serve in a local church when we are "home", and being willing to serve family, in addition to clients, while living nomadically in the ministry's RV. It's a lifestyle choice, not a convenience choice. All in or all out; hot or cold, not lukewarm. It isn't easy, nor what we would choose for enjoyment's sake. And it definitely doesn't fall in the boundaries of our original preconceived expectations, but it is where He's called us. We simply have the ability in His strength to continue to say, "Yes, I'll go wherever You lead; no ifs."

What about you? Are there places that you recognize you've limited, conditionally surrendering to God? If so, are you willing to shift to a place that embodies, "I'll surrender, no matter what, Lord" in both word and deed? He'll walk with you each step. He's just waiting for you to step into unconditional trust and submission to His will.

Originally posted on www.bluefirelegacy.org by Dallas Henslee on 04/01/22

My Mud Hut on Wheels

"Go therefore and make disciples of all nations...."
(Matthew 28:19, ESV)

When I was younger, we visited Heritage Park in Calgary, Alberta. There were parts of the park that I really enjoyed and others that I didn't. I loved the old-time candy store and ice cream shop. What kid wouldn't? I *didn't* love experiencing the sod shack/mud hut by stepping inside. I found it stuffy, closed in, and dark. It made it hard to breathe. Fast forward many years ... Now, I have my own mud hut, which I share with Mark and our dog, Ginger.

Not How I Roll

Mark and I spent a period of time homeless and couch-surfing at the onset of founding Blue Fire Legacy. Numerous generous friends and family provided beds, showers, and laundry facilities during this time (some of which was akin to long-term camping). In November 2021, we sold the house that we were finally able to buy previously, to end this homeless period. Since the sale of the house, we have been living in a 5th wheel trailer.

For me, our trailer (aka home and ministry office) is my mud hut on wheels. When I surrendered my life to ministry at 16, I had no concept that it might look like this. When God didn't seem to be tugging on my heart to move internationally, I was relieved. Smugly I assumed, "Home missions it is" … with all the comforts and amenities I was used to. God had other plans. Hard plans even. Of course, the reality is that we do both home and international ministry now. Sometimes, we do so in person, boots on the ground, and more frequently, virtually through the technology that permits us to work with individuals, groups, or church communities in faraway lands.

Plenty of people choose to live this way, RVing full-time, for the sheer adventure of it. They enjoy seeing how minimalistic they can live while traveling to visit various sites and attractions along the way. The novelty of constant change is invigorating to them. Others enjoy the simpler living space and take advantage of spending many hours outdoors. That just isn't *quite* how I roll.

Our Own Tiny Space

This go around of finding ourselves without a house, we have our own space … it's simply small and mobile. There are extra challenges with working and living in such a small space. Have you ever noticed how loud you are, even when trying to be quiet? Grabbing a quick snack, heating something up to eat or drink, doing the dishes or other quick cleaning task, rustling papers, etc. can all be quite a distraction, when your spouse is attempting to meet with a client, sometimes half the world away, all while sitting mere inches from you.

I see our RV as my mud hut because meeting with people isn't a job for me. It is a lifestyle of being completely called apart and dependent on the Lord; dependent for our well-being, financial provision, and scheduling. No, I don't have cobras or venomous insects to be concerned about; but somewhere, in a spot we have yet to discover, the bees have found an opening to be able to come inside. Yes, I have water and electricity (though the hot water runs out quickly), but I'm also removed from consistent support systems. Uprooting on a regular basis to travel to our next designated spot lends to feelings of instability and loneliness at times.

Hidden Costs and Benefits

Recently someone asked me how I was adjusting to the RV life. I responded by saying, "It is a lifestyle of obedience rather than preference."

There are hidden costs to embracing the call of God on your life. Sometimes, you're the consistent one, so people forget you need encouragement. Other times, the faithful are taken for granted and overlooked or dismissed with thoughts like, "Oh, they'll understand if I don't make it or back out." Holidays and celebrations are more difficult to coordinate when you don't have space to entertain family and friends. Days and nights of intercession for and crying over clients and their ministry difficulties adds an added layer to your own burdens carried consistently before the Lord.

There are also benefits of embracing the call. A real time testimony to those walking out their journey with you. Strengthening and discipling those younger or less mature in their faith. "Street cred" to minister to those struggling to walk out their callings. The benefit of the peace and satisfaction of "Yes and amen" in growing with the Lord in what He designed for you to do.

Not everyone is called to vocational ministry. Not everyone is called to immerse themselves in a foreign culture. Maybe your mud hut is your community or job. You will still have opportunities to minister to those in your circles. Your mud hut may be a figurative or metaphorical vehicle that positions you to minister in a specific circle. My mud hut just happens to be an actual vehicle on wheels.

The Great Commission

"Go therefore and make disciples of all nations, baptizing them in the name of the Father and of the Son and of the Holy Spirit, teaching them to observe all that I have commanded you. And behold, I am with you always, to the end of the age." (Matthew 28:19-20, ESV)

Originally posted on www.bluefirelegacy.org by Dallas Henslee on 03/11/22

4
Reflecting the Light

Reflecting a Kaleidoscope of Joy and Love

"Every good gift and every perfect gift is from above, coming down from the Father of lights, with whom there is no variation or shadow due to change." (James 1:17, ESV)

As I was waiting for our luggage to arrive in the baggage claim area, I looked up and saw a man with a mustache and tattoos all over his neck and head. I realized after looking a bit longer, that it was a face hood/gaiter mask. It made me immediately think of how easy it is to look one way on the outside but completely different inside.

In our ministry, we teach about markers. Usually, we are referring to something in the spirit realm that makes you an easier target for the enemy. We share that this concept is a twisting and perversion of the mark that God put on Cain as a protective identifier.

In current times, there is great discussion about what constitutes the mark of the beast referenced in Revelation. In addition, there are debates as to whether we are currently being conditioned to more easily agree to receive the mark.

As Christians, there is reason to resist the mark of the beast, but we are to be marked. The marks may be born physically on our bodies from being tortured for simply proclaiming Christ as Lord, or it could be a more subtle mark as people realize there is something different about us. What is inside shines through and impacts those around us in thought, in word, and in deed.

Galatians 6:17b, ESV, says, "... for I bear on my body the marks of Jesus."

Reflections of Color

I have a pair of flip-flops, or slippers if you prefer, that are decorated with cut plastic beads that sparkle. They're pretty to look at, but when the sun catches those sandals at just the right angle, it shines through the beads and projects a kaleidoscope effect on nearby walls and various surfaces. Beauty is then infused with joy. Of course, I play with that kaleidoscope effect when it happens and make the colors dance just for the fun of it. The light accentuates the beauty.

During our ministry trip, we had the opportunity to spend a few hours at the beach. While we were enjoying ourselves on the beach during our day of rest, I noticed how the light in the sky accentuated the color variations in the ocean. Clear, turquoise, blue, dark blue with precise demarcations of where each color started and stopped. Then the clouds rolled in and the dark sky impacted the water's beauty. Suddenly, all the water looked gray and blah.

That can happen to us, too. We are called to be salt and light to the world, and we try. We give it a valiant effort until some storm comes rolling in. Suddenly, our disposition isn't so carefree and sunny. We're moody or explosive around others, and we start to look blah and not so attractive to those around us.

"Every good gift and every perfect gift is from above, coming down from the Father of lights, with whom there is no variation or shadow due to change." (James 1:17, ESV)

God does not vary depending on His mood. Therefore, as we become more Christ-like, it stands to reason that we would be able to more consistently, without variation, allow His Light to shine from us.

Allowing His Light to Shine Through Us

When we submit ourselves to Him and allow His Light to pass through us, consistency, an unoffendable spirit, and truthfulness are characteristics we display. We put off the old or false self.

"Do not lie to one another, seeing that you have put off the old self with its practices and have put on the new self, which is being renewed in knowledge after the image of its creator." (Colossians 3:9-10, ESV)

I can only assume that the man under the gaiter/hood looks completely different underneath the printed band of cloth. For some, this disconnect or contrast, like the mask versus reality, is how they perceive the church. In other words, they can't get past the outward appearance to see if there is anything attractive, and they use this as an indictment against us. They see what is most obvious on the outside, because we have not put away the old self adequately.

We need to submit ourselves to the purifying fire of the Holy Spirit so that those that have accused us of being false and disingenuous see the love of God flowing through us. Scripture says they will know us by our love. Where do you have the opportunity to share love with those that are hard to love?

Do We Accurately Reflect Christ?

When others look at us, do they see Him? My prayer is that they not only see Him, but that they also feel the fruit of the Spirit, especially love.

"But the fruit of the Spirit is love, joy, peace, patience, kindness, goodness, faithfulness, gentleness, self-control; against such things there is no law." (Galatians 5:22-23, ESV)

"So now faith, hope, and love abide, these three; but the greatest of these is love." (1 Corinthians 13:13, ESV)

Originally posted on www.bluefirelegacy.org by Dallas Henslee on 08/07/20

Walk with the Light of the World

"The light shines in the darkness, and the darkness has not overcome it." (John 1:5, ESV)

I was visiting with a friend when she shared with me that her bird went through a season of not singing. She said she wasn't certain the cause or if there were even multiple causes, but she had concluded that he needed to spend more time in the light each day.

Her bird is really pretty - or I suppose I should say *handsome* given that he's male. His vibrant yellow appearance compliments his outgoing nature. He usually really likes to participate in conversations when other people are around, so much so that he can get loud enough for her to cover his cage to get him to be quiet. It is uncharacteristic for him to go days or weeks without singing.

We Need More Light

When she shared her theory of "Birdie" needing more light each day, I was thinking, *there's a spiritual truth here.* We need the Light. The Light gives us joy despite circumstances and a voice to dispel the darkness. The joy of the Lord is our strength. (Nehemiah 8:10)

Sunlight helps regulate our mood and sleep cycles. In the world of psychotherapy, artificial sources of light are used to imitate sunlight and treat depression amongst other diagnoses. Exposure to sunlight communicates to our bodies to create the appropriate production of hormones. Without light, plants cannot grow. Without Jesus, The Light, our spirits also experience an inability to grow and thrive.

Adjust Your Focus

Part of what Mark and I do is to teach on spiritual warfare. We often caution people to protect their focus. It's easy to see darkness and become fearful or have your joy snuffed out. (We know this is so because we are required to live out lessons before we can teach them to others.) When dealing with spiritual darkness, we need to focus on bringing the Light of Jesus into the situation, not on the oppression of the darkness.

Having joy despite the circumstances and getting exposed to enough Light is the only way we are still singing. It doesn't make earthly sense to be able to praise in a place of brokenness, dependence, or the unknown. We have found that when we choose to praise *despite* our emotions, we can see the Light better. Not only can we see the Light better, but we can feel the healing and encouragement the Light of the World offers us.

"Again Jesus spoke to them, saying, 'I am the light of the world. Whoever follows me will not walk in darkness, but will have the light of life.'" (John 8:12, ESV)

Light in the Darkness

Each of us have gone through seasons that were difficult. I probably relate to "Birdie" differently than you, but we each have our dark seasons.

I recall a time when I was elated to report to someone that I had actually felt the urge to sit at the piano and pour out my heart in song and instrumental worship, which I hadn't done in several years. My focus had shifted to the darkness, even though the Light was still present.

We had come through a time in ministry when it seemed as if no one wanted anything to do with us. We had lost our ministry, our church family, our friends, and family life was pretty bleak.

Eventually, the desire for a deeper relationship with the Lord increased, crowding out the hurt and disappointment of our past. I was able to sing and engage in creativity again. Then my song gained strength and joy. I was going to need that in the future. Of course, I didn't recognize it at the time. I was simply reveling in the ability to enjoy music again.

"The light shines in the darkness, and the darkness has not overcome it." (John 1:5, ESV)

Focused on the Light

Fast-forward several years. We had just sold our home. It was spacious and decorated to our preferences. It was the only house our three kids remember growing up in. Selling our home didn't come with the promise of moving into another one. In fact, at this point in our lives, Mark and I had committed to going into full-time ministry without the benefit of assured income. Eventually, we were able to purchase a small place, but only after God took us through some hard lessons. In these, we learned that He would be faithful, and that He was THE Provider. We held on to this when we were homeless for fifty-four weeks. We held on to it when a business deal went south and cost us a bundle. We held on to it when He asked us to surrender the remaining finances in our bank account. The difference from the first time we went through the dark valley to this time was that we knew to look for the Light rather than accept the illusion of complete darkness.

We Can Sing

We still hold onto His unchanging, never-failing character. We find it easier to sing in the face of the darkness, because we know that God is our Refuge. He is our Defender and Victor. He is the Light. We can sing, because we are looking for the Light each step of the way.

Are you living in the light or wandering in the dark? Regardless of the circumstances of life, you can have joy in the Light of the World.

"Your word is a lamp to my feet and a light to my path." (Psalm 119:105, ESV)

Originally posted on www.bluefirelegacy.org by Dallas Henslee on 03/01/19

Shine Bright in the Darkness of the World

"In the same way, let your light shine before others, so that they may see your good works and give glory to your Father who is in heaven." (Matthew 5:16, ESV)

From the patio outside the apartment we are staying in, I can see a lighthouse out on the far bluff. I did some research and have found out that Hams Bluff Lighthouse has not been in operation since the mid-1990s. The lighthouse was built by the Danish and first lit in 1915. When the Danish West Indies were transferred to the United States in 1917, the responsibilities for the lighthouse were shifted to the United States Lighthouse Service and later to the US Coast Guard.

Today, Hams Bluff Lighthouse sits on the northwest corner of St. Croix, USVI unused, rusting away. A visit to the bluff allowed me to see firsthand the rust and decay that is occurring. Climbing up the ladder and standing on the rusted floor full of holes and missing sections is not for the faint of heart.

There is a new tower that was put up about 10 years ago that flashes a light in the night as the need is still there for the safety of the boats that travel these waters. But it is a mere skeleton (literally) of the original.

A Beacon of Hope and Safety

A lighthouse can be seen for miles around through the dark nights. It provides a beacon of hope for sailors navigating the waters. There is safety in the warning of the flashing beam from the shore.

I was told by one Cruzan sailor that Hams Bluff Lighthouse saved his life. This from a man who was born here and has sailed around the island his entire life. I'm sure that there are thousands of stories about how a lighthouse saved sailors from crashing on the rocks and shorelines that would have broken their boats and caused great harm.

In so many ways, the Church is much like the lighthouses built on bluffs around the world. We are to provide a beacon of hope in the dark, dangerous world. We are to shine the light of Jesus Christ, guiding the people of the world to a safe harbor.

A Changed Focus

As navigation tools have changed and become more modern, lighthouses are becoming viewed as less important. With GPS, sailors can navigate the dark waters with a sense of safety and no longer look for the flashing lights.

Similarly, the world is no longer looking to the Church to help them navigate life. Society used to be centered around the local church. Today, a relative few look to the church for hope and safety. The buildings still stand, but many of them are a mere shell of what they used to be because the Light is no longer shining from within.

The Church has largely given its responsibilities of feeding the poor, caring for the widows and orphans, and caring for the community around it to the government. We have become a gathering place for the few. A sense of importance but lacking the substance that the world needs.

Unfortunately, we have too often chosen to live as the world instead of calling the world to a better life. Ephesians 5:7-14 tells us that we need to be walking as "children of light" and expose that which hides in the darkness.

We Need to be Shining Lights

People all around us need the Light of the World (Jesus Christ) more than ever today. The only way they will ever see it is if the Church shines bright in the darkness.

The Church should be a body of believers working together in Christlikeness, reaching out to the world, providing hope and safety. The Church is not a building, nor just the elders and leaders in the church. All of the followers of Christ make up the Church, which includes you and me. Reaching the world starts with each one of us personally determining to live as imitators of Christ. With sacrificial love, Christ gave His life so we can live. Are we willing to sacrifice our personal desires, opinions, and comfort so that the world can have eternal life?

Instead of debating which songs we should be singing or what program meets my preferences, we should start caring for the widows and orphans. We need to be lifting up the poor and providing a way out of poverty. The Church is instructed to make disciples of Christ. Too often, we are found coddling each other like entitled members in a country club.

Shine Bright

We don't need the best light show, we need to be the light shining outside of the church. If a lighthouse shines its light only inside itself, there would be no reason for its existence. The church must be shining in the darkness of the world around it.

It starts with me and you. Are we shining bright in the darkness?

"You are the light of the world. A city set on a hill cannot be hidden. Nor do people light a lamp and put it under a basket, but on a stand, and it gives light to all in the house. In the same way, let your light shine before others, so that they may see your good works and give glory to your Father who is in heaven." (Matthew 5:14-16, ESV)

Originally posted on www.bluefirelegacy.org by Mark Henslee on 07/24/20

5
Identity Issues

The Plague of the Never-ending Finish

> *"For the moment all discipline seems painful rather than pleasant, but later it yields the peaceful fruit of righteousness to those who have been trained by it."* (Hebrews 12:11, ESV)

I have an entrepreneurial spirit which is great for coming up with ideas or better ways of doing things. It is fun to dream, analyze, and contemplate the possible ways of doing something. Jumping into a new project is exciting and invigorating. But how about when the going gets tough, or when we have to drudge through some less than pleasant task? How we complete something is probably more important than how we start.

Among the many things that I enjoy is home renovations and building stuff. I'm good at starting projects but not as good about finishing them. How many of you have a task list (on paper or just in your head) that includes items related to projects that you started with zeal but have since languished?

An Example of One of My Projects

We owned a house for about 17 years. In the course of those years, I landscaped the entire lot, completed the basement, and renovated almost all of the rooms in the house in some form or fashion. There were times that I would want to jump to the next project without completing the current one. This could create stress in the house.

I remember the Friday that I came home from work and found that Dallas had pulled up the carpet from the stairs. You see, I had put in new hardwood flooring upstairs and tile downstairs with the plan to combine the two on the stairs. Well, after a several month delay, Dallas determined that it was time to get it done. What better way of motivating me to get going than to pull up the carpet on a Friday afternoon?

I had my reasons for not completing the project: I hadn't figured out just how to get the tile to be the exact same height as the hardwood; the trim wasn't fully clear in my mind; it was a lot of cutting tile and pieces of wood; it wasn't that bad to still have the old carpet there (if you ignore the visual aesthetic); and probably some other reasons just because there is always one more.

Just like me, I'm betting that you have a list of reasons that your project (dare I say projects?) isn't completed. The reality is that it boils down to priorities. What we value the most is what will get our time, energy and resources. Often, what we say we value doesn't quite make the list in practice.

The Cost of Unfinished Projects

Unfortunately, when we have unfinished projects or things that need done hanging over our heads, we carry additional stress. The toll that it places on us is higher than we probably realize. There is a mental cost (ever wake up in the middle of the night thinking about it?), an emotional price (the drain of knowing we are disappointing someone, even if it is just ourselves), and often a relational toll (family and friends that see the incomplete items and may become frustrated and let us know just how disappointed they are in us).

It has taken a lot of years for me to learn how to deal with the issue of unfinished things. I can't say that it is easy or that I'm always good about actually doing it, but I'm much improved from the old ways.

A Process for Getting It Done

Here are some helpful suggestions for how to get those unfinished things on our task list completed and behind us.

Write it down

Make a list of all of the unfinished projects that you have in your life. This may be a very daunting realization when you see them all on paper, but do not give in to the fear of the magnitude of the task. The only way to eat an elephant is one bite at a time. You will be able to complete your list one task at a time.

Prioritize

Once you have your list, even if it is unreasonably long, you need to go through and prioritize the projects. If you are married, I highly suggest that there be a discussion of the importance of each project. If your wife has been living with an unfinished bathroom for a couple years, that may take priority over completing the shelves in your garage.

Part of the process of prioritizing may require that you estimate the amount of time or money required for each. We all have limited time and resources (money) and some things take more of one or another. A side note for the future – don't start a project that you don't have the resources to complete in a reasonable amount of time.

Determine the steps needed

Once you have prioritized your projects, take the first few and determine the individual steps needed to complete them. It should be a relatively detailed breakdown, but don't get lost in the minutiae. Remember that elephant? By breaking a project up into steps, it becomes more manageable. It also will give you some encouragement as you start crossing things off your list.

Schedule

Put it on the calendar or at least put a time frame for completing each step. Time is really good at slipping through our fingers. We generally do good at making time to go to work and eat meals. Some of us even make sure we get adequate sleep each night. Make the time in your schedule to complete those things that are hanging out unfinished.

The biggest struggle here is that you may overschedule yourself. We naturally think it will take less time than in reality. Allow for the likelihood that not everything will go as smoothly as hoped. As a general rule of thumb, take the amount of time you think it will take and double or triple it. If you are more efficient, you can pat yourself on the back and move to the next task sooner.

Just do it

Now that you have made your list, prioritized, broken it down into steps and scheduled a time, you have to pick up the tools and get to it. Put down the distractions, set aside the excuses and get started.

Once you start, it generally isn't nearly as bad as you had built it up to be. I find that getting going on finishing something is almost as good as when the project was new. And as you work, you get to cross things off the task list.

Celebrate

As you complete each of the previously unfinished projects, there should be some form of celebration. For the smaller ones, it may simply be a cold drink and a few minutes of sitting on the couch. For the bigger projects, take the wife and / or family and enjoy something together to celebrate.

As you work down the list of projects, you will probably begin to feel a sense of accomplishment and also a reduced burden of the undone. The family will be thrilled to not have to walk through the unfinished space. Friends may start to look at you differently, even with an awe or envy about your prowess of completing things. And you will be able to look yourself in the mirror knowing that you finished well!

"Whatever you do, work heartily, as for the Lord and not for men…." (Colossians 3:23, ESV).

Originally posted on www.bluefirelegacy.org by Mark Henslee on 10/05/18

Stung by the Plague of Busyness

"It is in vain that you rise up early and go late to rest, eating the bread of anxious toil; for he gives to his beloved sleep."
(Psalm 127:2, ESV)

Many times over the years I've been accused of being a "workaholic". It started when I was a teenager and continued through much of my adult life. While I generally denied the accusations, they were not without merit.

My senior year in high school, I worked three jobs in addition to maintaining straight A's in school. While completing my degrees in accounting (BS and MS), I worked full-time, had a family, and went to school in the evenings. As a CPA, it was common for me to clock 2400 to 2600 hours per year with tax season being 60 to 80 hours per week. Many of those years, I was also pastoring a church or working in some other ministry role. I generally have not shied away from hard work and long hours.

A Pandemic of Busyness

I'm not the only one who has a tendency to stay busy. As we talk with people around the world, it is exceedingly common for them to be too busy to keep up with everything they have to do. I'm guessing that many of you can relate to this feeling. We are a busy world.

And if you are waiting for retirement to not be busy, you may be disappointed. A large percentage of retired people that I meet are just as busy, or busier, than when they worked regular jobs. A common saying is, "I don't know how I had time for a job."

It's interesting to me that we have all kinds of technology that was supposed to give us more time, and yet, we seem to be busier than ever before. With each new invention, instead of slowing down, we keep speeding up. Expecting more and more productivity.

We work from home, or the car, or the beach while supposedly on vacation. We're so plugged in that we are frying our circuits.

The Perceived Benefits of Busyness

There are some benefits to being busy. We get things done, producing and earning a living. We may feel a sense of accomplishment, and yet, many people are *less* satisfied with what they've accomplished.

We appear to be important because we do so many things. This is especially true in the church. We can be so busy *serving* God that we fail to have a *relationship* with Him.

Some of us stay busy to avoid things such as hurts or difficult situations. This really is not a benefit but rather a detriment of busyness. I was really good at this tactic. As a teenager, it was better to be working than to face the imperfections of my family life. I found my value in work and good grades. I continued this pattern well into adulthood.

It is easier to stay busy than to face our emotions. If I ask a guy how he is doing with the emotional turmoil of a difficult situation, it is common to get a response along the lines of, "I'm staying busy." In other words, "I'm avoiding facing those feelings by working or keeping occupied all of the time." Unfortunately, the situations that are being avoided do not just go away. Sweep enough stuff under the rug, and eventually you will be tripping on the mountainous rug.

Busy with the Right Things

Laziness is not the antidote to busyness. In fact, there are several Proverbs that speak against slothfulness (A few references are Proverbs 10:26, 15:19, 18:9, 19:15). It is important that we work and are productive. We need to be doing the things that we are supposed to be doing and not the other things that just keep us busy.

Our first board member said, "There are a lot of good things. You are not called to all of them." This has been a valuable reminder for us the past five plus years. Just because something is good, does not mean that I am the one who is supposed to be doing it. In fact, we may be stealing from others if we do what they are called to do, instead of stepping back and allowing them to step up.

Many of us struggle with a certain two letter word. "No" is so hard to say when we see a person in need or we're asked to help with this or that. There's a common saying about staying in our lanes. We need to be doing our stuff, not other people's. Sometimes, we have to say, "No" to the good things so that we can say, "Yes" to the best things.

Be Still and Know God

How do we know what the right things are for us to be doing? We have to slow down enough to spend time with the Lord and hear from Him what is ours to do. For us workaholics, slowing down is a lot harder to do than we may want to admit. Sitting in silence is akin to torture for many of us. And yet, that is what is required.

The reward for adjusting our life to align with the Lord's instructions for us is priceless. Many think that we went off the rails and have lost our minds with the shift we made to follow God. Yes, there are some things that I miss about the old ways. I also have to face my emotions and struggles head on instead of burying myself in work.

Regardless of what we've given up, I don't ever want to go back. A weekly Sabbath is a necessity in life now, and it is good. I'm closer to Dallas and the Lord. You can't put a value on what I have today that I was missing because I was busy.

Be still. Sounds easy, but it isn't. Are you willing to stop long enough to truly listen? When the Lord tells you what you should and shouldn't be doing, are you willing to make the changes in life? If you will, I promise it will be worth it.

"Be still, and know that I am God." (Psalm 46:10a, ESV)

Originally posted on www.bluefirelegacy.org by Mark Henslee on 05/21/21

Bloom Where You Are Transplanted

"And whatever you do, in word or deed, do everything in the name of the Lord Jesus, giving thanks to God the Father through him." (Colossians 3:17, ESV)

There is a saying that many of us are familiar with that simply says, "Bloom where you're planted." It graces bumper stickers, window decals, plaques for your walls, steppingstones for your garden, and journals. It may even have colorful flowers and a contrasting border to aesthetically emphasize the motto. On the surface, it sounds like good advice.

While it is an encouraging sentiment, as I began to ponder it, I found that it lacked a fullness of truth. We tend to toss this pop psychology around, when circumstances are difficult or undesirable, in an effort to make the best of a situation.

Bloom

Bloom—absolutely! Take stock of the environment and expectations and utilize what you can to enhance where you've been placed for that season.

I find the breakdown in fullness occurs around "...where you are planted." Some take this to the extreme, meaning one should never desire change or to better their station in life. This falls in line with a caste system or a very restrictive, possibly to the point of being oppressive, way of thought that embeds religions as well as cultures.

If our biblical heroes had followed this advice, they would not have been able to carry out the Great Commission. Consider the interplay of the Great Commission and the words prior to Jesus' ascension taken together regarding "going". The combination of the instructions indicates that going into further regions is imperative.

"Go therefore and make disciples of all nations, baptizing them in the name of the Father and of the Son and of the Holy Spirit, teaching them to observe all that I have commanded you. And behold, I am with you always, to the end of the age." (Matthew 28:19-20, ESV)

"But you will receive power when the Holy Spirit has come upon you, and you will be my witnesses in Jerusalem and in all Judea and Samaria, and to the end of the earth."
(Acts 1:8, ESV)

Where Transplanted

It has been my experience that sometimes a plant needs to be transplanted. Sometimes for the health or natural maturation of the plant, and other times for the sake of enhanced eye appeal. See, seeds which grow into fragile shoots may need to be hardened off to withstand various weather conditions. The conditioned sprouts are then transplanted so they can continue to grow and produce.

Other times, plants are growing too closely together and begin to crowd or have needs for more nutrients in the soil. In such instances, the plant is not moved to increase production, but to offer a space where it can better thrive.

Just like plants, God can move us. He may move us to strengthen a character trait. Perhaps it's because our giftings are needed elsewhere, and sometimes He moves us out of a difficult situation because someone else is disobedient. In those instances, He's conserving our energy and protecting our hearts.

Be Adaptive

We shouldn't despair or run because something is difficult. We should embrace where He has us for *that* season.

What if Joseph refused to adapt to each new circumstance? Or Moses? Or Paul? It requires adaptation to move between surviving and thriving.

In Joseph's case, dealing with hardship and adapting for each season meant going from being the favored son to being sold into slavery, gaining some station to work under Potiphar to then be imprisoned, again finding a measure of favor and helping to run the prison while remaining a prisoner, to then serving under Pharaoh.

In Moses' case, it meant being born during a time male babies were being killed and then being adopted into the Pharaoh's family by his daughter. Privilege was turned into exile when he let his rage go so far as to murder an Egyptian and yet, we largely think of the leadership Moses carried out. There were seasons of adaptation and growth in each set of circumstances.

Or how about Paul? The revered apostle who went from persecuting Christians to discipling them being himself persecuted, imprisoned, and surviving numerous trials and life-threatening circumstances. Paul didn't stay in one place hoping to bloom only by writing instructions. Rather, he traveled extensively!

Choose to Bloom

Yes, I absolutely believe God is sovereign and has a purpose for our lives. I believe that He stations us, just as He stationed the heroes of our faith; moving us out of our comfort zones even to the point of calling us to move to other countries to serve as missionaries.

I believe that in each station, He not only has growth for us, but also, joy in the journey as we learn to embrace the circumstances, find joy despite the circumstances, and share this joy by seeing people through His eyes even to the point of loving the "unlovable". It is in this respect, I feel that we are to walk in faith and obedience and *bloom wherever He transplants us* so that we can fulfill His directive to be salt and light to the world.

Originally posted on www.bluefirelegacy.org by Dallas Henslee on 08/10/18

A Glimpse of a Father and Son and What Relationship Could Be

"See what kind of love the Father has given to us, that we should be called children of God; and so we are..."

(1 John 3:1, ESV)

My father and I had a rather distant connection for the past 30 or so years. In many ways, we were estranged, though it seems strange to call it that. Mostly, we just didn't talk or connect.

I last saw him in September of 2010 when my oldest daughter was looking at colleges, and we were in the area where he lived. We met at a restaurant with my older brother and his family, along with dad and his second wife. We were a fairly large group, so not much was discussed other than the events of the day.

Why didn't we talk? Well, I'm not really certain the real reason. He left my mom when I was in college, and the connection was never re-established after that. The first decade we had more interaction. He came to my wedding, which none of my siblings can claim. He met my kids when they were young, though they don't remember it. When I visited my

Mom, we would try to get together with Dad as well, though it had to be on my initiative.

A Title or a Name

Regardless of the connection, I have always called him Dad. For many people, that name denotes a relationship that is personal, and special. For me, it was really like any other name of a person.

I could have called him Ken, but that seemed weird. I grew up calling him Dad, so that was his name. When telling others about him, I would refer to him as "My Dad." Seemingly, as if there was a personal connection with him that was mine. But for the title or name used, we didn't have a relationship.

I'm not sure he knew most of the things of importance to me in life. He did know that I love Jesus and serve Him, though that wasn't something he celebrated. I know the general complaint, though I'm not sure exactly what happened. He was deeply hurt by the church. Therefore, my belief and life seemed to be hurtful to him.

Relationship is a Two-Way Street

For me, a relationship is a shared life. Two people that interact on a regular, ongoing basis. Both investing time, energy, effort, and emotion into the other person. Some relationships are closer than others, but they all have that shared investment.

Looking back at the last 30 years, I see several times that I could have done things differently with my Dad. Why didn't I? Sometimes, I was just too angry to make the effort. Other times, I was selfish and wanted him to reach out. No good reasons, just the reality of two imperfect men missing out on what could have been.

When I tried, he didn't respond. So why keep trying? I quit for a while. But the last few years I have attempted to reconnect. Maybe I could have done more. Maybe it wouldn't have mattered how much I did. I'll never know. The reality is that we didn't have a relationship.

There were definitely years that I did not invest any effort in my Dad. I had my hurts and issues that, for too long, I held against him. When I truly learned about forgiveness and did the hard work required, I was able to see Dad in a different way.

I began sending Father's Day cards and Christmas cards, and even remembered his birthday with a card a few times. I can only assume that he received all these cards because there was never an acknowledgement of them. I realize that I grieved my loss of him every year, as I stood in the card aisle.

Grieving What Wasn't

I'm not sure when I started grieving. The first several years, I was just mad for how he left and the hurt he caused my mom and siblings. It was a lot of work to deal with what he had done, and especially what he had not done, and come to a place of forgiveness.

Grief is a strange thing. Each of my siblings is grieving differently as we are all in a different place with losing Dad. I've been grieving him for a very long time. My grief now seems inappropriately small, but then I realize that I've done a lot of grieving him for years.

The other day, I spoke to Dad on the phone. He was lucid and knew who I was, unlike the time I called a couple months ago. I told him some about my kids and what they were doing. No real interest in my life, so I kept the sharing shallow. The call ended strangely. No goodbyes, just talking and then his step-daughter was on the phone.

Dallas asked how I was doing after the call. The only description I could come up with was "ambivalent." Not sad, not emotional, just a wonder of it being strange. That's not how it should be when a son talks to his father who is dying. Is something wrong with me? I should feel something, right?

I hope that my siblings don't interpret where I am as not caring. I care a lot. It just looks different than the normal son when his father dies. I guess I'm not normal, though I've not claimed to be for most of my life.

Viewing God Through Earthly Lenses

When we think about God the Father, we often view Him through the lens of our human relationships. Obviously, if I look at my heavenly Father the same way as my earthly father, I'm going to have a wrong view. But it's what we know, so it seems to be common.

Father God wants to walk in relationship with us. He wants to have a two-way interaction. Investing in us as we invest in Him. Talking regularly, sharing our feelings and emotions, asking questions and listening to responses, being involved in the big and small things.

Sometimes, we walk away and think that He doesn't want to participate in our life. We may get angry about something He allowed to happen. We may even blame Him for causing the painful event.

There are times when we cry out, and it seems like silence coming back. I don't know why it is like that at times. I've experienced those times of silence. They are hard; so very hard. It seems uncaring and harsh. Things that are not in God's character.

Beloved Child

What do we do with the hurts of silence? Personally, I tend to throw a big tantrum and yell louder. I remember one time I had to pull off the road and just yell and scream at God. It was ugly in the car that day. At the end of my tantrum, I heard God quietly say, "I love you son." And that was it. No other answer, no explanation, no resolution. Just, "I love you son."

I've come to appreciate those words very deeply. While I would like an explanation, I'm thinking that I wouldn't understand even if He gave me one. My desire for resolution has given way to my simply being a beloved son. My true identity - a beloved son of God. What better position to be in than that of a beloved son?

Regardless of what happens in life, I know exactly who I am. There are so very many things that I don't understand. Many, many things that I think are wrong, or should be done differently. Yet, I know He is good, and I am His. He is God, and I am not. There is security in simply being a beloved child of the most high God.

Epilogue

Since writing the above post, my dad passed from this life on April 3, 2021. The Lord was exceedingly gracious and gave me another phone call with Dad prior to his passing. I got to tell him that I love him and say goodbye. He called me "son" and told me that he loved me. Precious words that I'd waited years to hear. That call ended with me in tears, not ambivalent. I trust he is in the mercy and grace of the Lord.

Originally posted on www.bluefirelegacy.org by Mark Henslee on 04/16/21

Receive the Father's Unconditional Love

"For while we were still weak, at the right time Christ died for the ungodly. For one will scarcely die for a righteous person—though perhaps for a good person one would dare even to die—but God shows his love for us in that while we were still sinners, Christ died for us."

(Romans 8:6-8, ESV)

We talk a lot about love in churches and families. Unfortunately, I think we often have distorted views of God's love based on our experiences with human versions of love. Today, I want to explore unconditional love.

A Father's Love

It was over 25 years ago, yet I can still remember very clearly the first time I held our oldest daughter. We were young, foolish, naive, and certainly not ready to be parents. But the moment that I held that precious little baby, I was changed forever. There aren't adequate words in the English language to describe the connection that I felt. The depth of love that I knew for her was beyond my understanding.

There have been times in the past 25 years that I didn't show that love perfectly. I didn't fully know how to put into action the love that was in my heart. I operated from my experiences and understanding. Yet, even in my mistakes and failures, I loved her.

Unearned Love

There is nothing that any of my kids can do to cause me to stop loving them. For you see, they didn't do anything to earn my love. Because they didn't earn it, they can't "unearn" it. (Yes, I know unearn isn't a proper word).

The Father's love is also unearned; we can't do anything to cause Him to stop loving us. Scripture tells us that He loves us so much that He gave His only Son that we might have life everlasting (John 3:16). And that great sacrifice was made while we were still sinners (Romans 5:8).

Yet, we seem to think that if we don't do everything just right, we won't have God's love. Say the wrong thing and you better be looking over your shoulder or duck to avoid that lightning bolt. That's not love, that's a dictator ruling by fear. God is NOT a dictator seeking to smite. He is a loving father seeking relationship with us.

A Skewed Perspective

I've been hanging around churches and Christians for over four decades now. I've seen a broad spectrum of beliefs and ways of applying the Bible to our everyday lives. Unfortunately, there are a lot of Christians and churches that have a very skewed concept of God's love.

One day, as a teenager, I was confronted after church by a gentleman. My "crime" that day (there were many in my teen years) was to wear a tie with jeans. Yes, he specifically called me out and told me that I should be wearing dress pants if I was going to wear a tie! Never mind the fact that I didn't own dress pants or that it was a knit tie which was commonly worn with jeans back then. Even though I went to the effort and discomfort of wearing a tie to church, because I wanted to honor the Lord, in his opinion, I was an insult to God.

Just as that gentleman had developed a wrong perspective of what is important, we often have many experiences in life that are causing us to not see God's love as it is. We read stories in the Bible about people being killed by God for seemingly innocent acts such as Uzzah who touched the Ark in 2 Samuel 6. These experiences have developed in us a skewed understanding of who God is and how much He really loves us.

Dark Days

Ten years ago, I was angry with God, the church, church people, and just about anyone else that got in my way. For about two years, I lived in a deep place of anger and bitterness. I told God that I didn't like His people, and I wasn't sure how I felt about Him. I quit church and was certainly never going to work in ministry again. Those were very dark days in my life.

In those days, I did everything I could to ignore God. Yet, much like the prodigal son, when I was willing to look back at Him, He was there. Not with a lecture about my behavior. Not with condemnation or shame. He was there with open arms and very clearly said "I love you, son."

Through the following days of restoration, as I struggled with who I am and who He is, the most frequent words I heard were "I love you, son." His love was always there. I am the one who walked away, hurt and angry. He never stopped loving me. He never stopped pursuing me.

Identity

In our ministry, we work with people who are called to minister. Most church folk think that ministers are near-perfect people who have life (and God) all figured out. At the risk of bursting a few bubbles, we are actually some of the most messed up people that you could imagine. Ministers often have backgrounds that include abuse, rejection, addictions, failures, and many other significant struggles.

How is it possible for someone with a broken life to be a minister? Through the incredible love of Father God!

When we accept our true identity as a child of God and receive His unconditional love, we become able to accomplish what He has called us to do. You see, it is not through our abilities, talents, efforts, or even doing the "right" things. The only way we can be successful and fulfilled is when we walk in His love and freely give that love to others in overflow.

Receiving Love

In general, we each operate through the biases of our understanding and experiences. If you grew up in a home that required you to perform to be accepted, then you will generally perform to gain acceptance as an adult. That may be in your work, your play, your religion, and your relationships. Not surprisingly, this impacts your relationship with God.

I want to encourage you to step outside of your understanding and experiences to receive the Father's love. God's love is more perfect than any love that we could ever have for another. The depth and breadth of our Heavenly Father's love is beyond our comprehension and understanding. There is nothing that you can do to earn His love, so stop trying. There is nothing you can do to lose His love, so stop thinking you can (Romans 8:39).

Just receive it. Invite Him to tell you how much He loves you. Allow Him to give you a hug. Give yourself permission to be a child, held by your loving Father. Experience His acceptance. Hear Him say "I love you, my child."

Originally posted on www.bluefirelegacy.org by Mark Henslee on 01/18/19

Anxiety in a World of Unknowns and Confusion

"Humble yourselves, therefore, under the mighty hand of God so that at the proper time he may exalt you, casting all your anxieties on him, because he cares for you."

(1 Peter 5:6-7, ESV)

All of us may deal with feelings of anxiety occasionally, or maybe even on a regular basis. This past week, there have been a significant number of people who have expressed increased anxiety. The United States of America had an election with high passions on both sides. The final results of the election may not be truly known at this point. Even what is known may change, as it sounds like the courts will be involved, as well as recounts in some areas.

In addition to the election, the world is continuing to deal with the Coronavirus pandemic. It doesn't seem to matter what people and the governments do or don't do, it just keeps spreading.

How do we deal with the unknown? Even more importantly, how do we trust God when everything around us appears to be contrary to what we think or expect He would be doing or allowing?

Our Control

We like to think that we have control over life. We get to make choices that will have an impact on our life. So do other people, and their choices not only impact their life, but can also affect us. In the end, we really have little control over much of our life.

Take for example our finances. We think we control how much money we earn, but that assumes that we get the right job at the salary we expect. How do we get that job? We obtain the needed education and experience - that we can control. We also need to connect with the people that make the decisions to hire and determine pay structures. In other words, we can prepare all we want, but if we don't make the needed connections, we won't have the job.

We can also prepare a budget and tell every dollar where it will go each month. That works until the washing machine breaks, or the car needs an unexpected repair. Prices of items may change from what we expected. (Anybody else seeing food cost more this year?) Again, we can do some things to control our expenses and savings, but there are outside influences and events which remain out of our control.

Our ability to control the political decisions of our government is fairly minimal. We certainly have no control over the weather or natural disasters. We don't even have the ability to control our family. It seems like the things that we can't control have the biggest impact on our life.

Sovereignty of God

I've often had conversations with God about why He did this, allowed that, or didn't do something. Generally, my "Why?" questions don't get answered. Why is that? Well, He hasn't told me, but I suppose it's because He doesn't see the benefit in explaining Himself to me.

The Lord doesn't have to answer our questions or explain Himself. He is sovereign. However, we can know that He will not abandon us (Hebrews 13:5). We also can know that He is good, even when we don't understand, because that is a part of His character. God is love (1 John 4:7-10) and therefore, He cannot be unloving. He will never violate who He is, and that should give us comfort in the midst of this crazy world.

Not everything will be as we hope or expect. God will even allow bad things to happen to good people. This can create a lot of why-questions that will, most likely, go unanswered. How are we supposed to handle these things?

Trust Through Faith

Trust in the Lord. We can trust Him in the midst of the unknown because of who He is. You may be saying, "Mark, you don't know what He has allowed in my life." I feel you and relate to experiencing hurts and hardships. We all experience some level of difficulty, hurt, disappointment, or dissatisfaction as we live life.

He wants to walk through each and every one of those experiences with you. His desire is to journey through everything side by side. What an amazing, incomprehensible concept. The Creator of the universe wants to be with me, always!

How do we trust the Lord? It is only possible through faith. "Faith is the assurance of things hoped for, the conviction of things not seen" (Hebrews 11:1, ESV). How do we get this faith? First, ask the Lord for it. Then, as we journey with Him, we will be able to exercise the faith He gives. In time, it will grow more and more, like a muscle that is used for heavier weights and bigger things. Maybe your faith will one day be bigger than you realize, and you'll trust Him beyond the limits.

Be Anxious for Nothing

Through faith in the Lord of lords, we will be able to live without anxiety. There will still be hard things, and stuff that we don't understand. Not everything will be as we think it should. However, we will be able to continue walking forward, side by side, with the Father who knows, understands, is good, and loves us.

"Rejoice in the Lord always, again I say, rejoice. Let your reasonableness be known to everyone. The Lord is at hand; do not be anxious about anything, but in everything by prayer and supplication with thanksgiving let your requests be made known to God. And the peace of God, which surpasses all understanding, will guard your hearts and your minds in Christ Jesus." (Philippians 4:4-7, ESV)

Originally posted on www.bluefirelegacy.org by Mark Henslee on 11/13/20

Struggling to Walk in High Heels

"Therefore, since we are surrounded by so great a cloud of witnesses, let us also lay aside every weight, and sin which clings so closely, and let us run with endurance the race that is set before us, looking to Jesus, the founder and perfecter of our faith, who for the joy that was set before him endured the cross, despising the shame, and is seated at the right hand of the throne of God. Consider him who endured from sinners such hostility against himself, so that you may not grow weary or fainthearted."

(Hebrews 12:1-3, ESV)

The Disastrous Aerial

Several years ago, I broke my tibial plateau. We reference it as breaking my knee, but the kneecap itself was unaffected. Basically, it was a radial fracture, which my orthopedist called "impressive", caused as a result of one of my skis not releasing when I fell. I'm told the aerial was beautiful; it was just the landing that needed a little work.

In addition to pain management and lots of doctor appointments, recovery meant no weight bearing for four months, the use of crutches and a wheelchair, the use of a continuous passive motion machine (aka torture device) for eight hours a day, every day, for over a month, and *lots* of physical therapy appointments.

The Struggle of Learning to Walk Again

Physical therapy, as you can imagine, was less than pleasant; dare I say difficult. Measuring range of motion and working to rehabilitate my knee was a major undertaking. Once we could start working towards walking again, I was faced with the fact that my brain and leg muscles had temporarily forgotten how to communicate and cooperate with each other. Then came using a walker, walking backwards, etc. There were days it was a struggle!

In the course of working with clients, sometimes, I run into the thought pattern that being happy is the ultimate goal, and therefore, struggle, any struggle, is a curse. But, this perspective is an incomplete, egocentric, selfish, and unbiblical outlook.

Is Struggle a Curse?

I will concede that not all suffering has a purpose; some of it truly is a curse sent from the Destroyer to torment. However, God has the power to redeem suffering. The Bible says we can have joy, but happiness is not promised. The Bible also discusses suffering. For the joy set before Him, Christ endured or suffered the cross. For the full text, see Hebrews 12:2.

The belief that any and all suffering is a curse is based on the fact that there is a cost and pain involved in the process. Sin brought the curse of painful childbirth and the necessity of toil to produce from the land (Genesis 3:16-17). Salvation does not suspend the consequence of sin while we remain in our physical form on earth.

Sin brought death and disease, and from this perspective, suffering is indeed a curse. However, what about the joy of the child that is born or the fruit (or vegetables and grains) of one's labor in the field that provides sustenance that comes from enduring the suffering? Or even the butterfly that endures the struggle of the chrysalis, the bird that is strengthened by working out of the egg, the character that is molded in the tumultuous circumstances, and ultimately the salvation that was provided by our Savior enduring the torture of the cross and conquering death? It is hard to defend the argument that any and all suffering is bad when you look at these examples.

Inconveniently Enduring

Observing the instructions of my doctors was inconvenient. It was difficult to get around the house. It was hard to sleep on my back with my leg strapped into a machine. Not being independent was a hassle; however, the consequence of not enduring and following the prescribed course of action could be that the fracture would deepen and create a full break requiring surgery. That would mean beginning recovery time over again. No thanks.

One visit, my PT said, "We'll keep working to get you back out running and enjoying the outdoors." I quickly informed him that my goal, what made this worth it to me to keep pushing through the pain and suffering, was the potential of being able to wear my cute high heel shoes again.

You can attempt to avoid as much struggle as possible, but is that truly in your best interest? Are you sacrificing growth or improvement by doing so? If you look at your struggles more closely, is there a reward on the other side of enduring?

I had to struggle to walk again, but I wouldn't classify the effort as a curse. There was a reward waiting, even if it was just balancing on a cute pair of shoes again as I walked.

Originally posted on www.bluefirelegacy.org by Dallas Henslee on 10/25/19

Today, Today is a Really Hard Day:

The Ugly Cry that No One at Church Will See

"But I am not ashamed, for I know whom I have believed, and I am convinced that he is able to guard until that day what has been entrusted to me. Follow the pattern of the sound words that you have heard from me, in the faith and love that are in Christ Jesus. By the Holy Spirit who dwells within us, guard the good deposit entrusted to you."

(2 Timothy 1:12-14, ESV)

Unhealthy Expectations

There is this weird, unhealthy expectation that we must *always* put forward our best faces at church. NO. MATTER. WHAT.

Sometimes, you hear this referred to as one's "church face" or "mask". These imaginary coverings are particularly useful if you've just had an intense argument or "special moment" in the car on the way to church. You pull into the parking lot and everyone dons their pleasant voices and approachable faces.

This desire to be greeted by nonthreatening, inauthentic, and "plastic" countenances is often projected onto our pastors and leadership with exponentially unrealistic expectations. You know the ones that sound something like, "That's our pastor and his family. They're perfect. They're superhuman like the *Incredibles*. They're...." Well, you get the idea.

The reality of the matter is, they are human. They have a residence that needs to be kept clean, they may have pets or children that are in need of extra care or have demanding academic and extracurricular activity schedules, they have bad hair days, and days when their car breaks down. In other words, everything is not always perfect.

While this entry was written a while ago and then transformed into a blog, my hope is that the candor of the following personal journey account helps you better understand how to support your pastor and leaders. Additionally, if you find yourself with such a title, I pray you feel a little less alone on those really tough days.

Untold Burdens Weigh on Me

Today is a really hard day. It's a day you likely won't hear about in any update newsletter from us, or anyone else in ministry, for that matter. That's because we depend on donations from our supporters and our supporters want to hear good news and momentum reports. So, we filter.

Today, we came right up against bills needing to be paid and the amount needed wasn't in our checking account, nor was the tiny bit remaining in our savings enough to pay everything owed. We have been instructed to live a debt free lifestyle so the fact that God didn't provide extra donations stung; and it sent me into a tailspin or crisis of faith.

See, it isn't just the monthly bills, but I also have a daughter that will be getting married soon. Presumably, there will be two more weddings for daughters in the next few years, and I have absolutely no money to help with the cost of the festivities. This breaks my heart, because I've dreamed of providing beautiful weddings and receptions for my girls for a very long time now.

Today is a hard day because several ministry related items and appointments seem on hold, and we are struggling to find community and a church family. Which means much of our spiritual gifting is largely unused at the current time as well.

Questioning the Call

Today is a hard day because I look at all *that* and wonder why God asked us to move here; to move to this rural community that is much more to my husband's liking than mine; especially when I'm not seeing the result of our sacrifice and labor.

On days like today, I long for the beautiful home and financial security we had when we were both employed. That time before God asked us to leave our "fishing nets" to come follow Him into full-time, solely donor supported ministry and exhaust our financial storehouses.

Today is hard because I have come to realize that we no longer live in a nation that says, "If I can't go, I'll support someone who can with my money." Instead, many now have an attitude of,

"Even though I can't serve on the mission field, I'm not convinced those who *are,* actually need my money."

All of that has brought me to today. A difficult day because in the last two months, I've had multiple friends lose parents, and watched another friend lose someone close to cancer. I've made an emergency trip to visit my own father in the hospital. In the midst of all that grief going on, I hear about summer vacations and date nights, and that just isn't part of my reality right now or foreseeable future.

The Floodgates Burst Open

Today was a hard day. It was hard enough that I couldn't keep my emotions contained anymore. I cried for hours. I simply could not stop. I couldn't eat dinner, and I just laid in bed asking God what I had missed, or what I was supposed to be doing. I was desperate enough to offer God the sacrifice of a fast that would look more like a hunger strike. I also confess I was dangerously close to giving up and deciding to live the remainder of my days without getting out of bed.

When your pastor or leaders tell you that your notes of encouragement are vital to those serving, whether near or far, they are *not* exaggerating! Part of what made today so hard was that I'm lonely, and I need to know someone outside my family still cares.

Today is a hard day because my husband and I each need friendships, mentors, and pastoral covering. As we look around, we find a void.

Today is a hard day because I must practice what I preach. I must stand against the lies of the enemy. I cannot allow myself to place my identity in what I do, and I cannot place my security in my finances.

BUT, I Hold Onto This Hope

Today is a hard day, but I have resolved to mirror Paul's convictions in 2 Timothy.

"...I know whom I have believed and am convinced that He is able to guard what I have entrusted to Him until that day." (2 Timothy 1:12, NIV)

Originally posted on www.bluefirelegacy.org by Dallas Henslee on 10/12/18

When Awe of the Extraordinary Fades to Common

Let every created thing give praise to the Lord, for He issued His command, and they came into being.

(Psalms 148:5, NLT)

Coming into our valley from the east, there are two places on the highway that give you incredible, awe-inspiring views. The first shows off the tops of the Sangre de Cristo Mountains. The second gives a panorama of the entire mountain range with the valley in full view. As one of my daughters would say: "Aaaawwwww!!!!!!".

Over the past couple of months, we have had a number of people visit us in beautiful Westcliffe, CO. We enjoy showing off the Lord's creation from our front door and especially from Prayer Rock at Legacy Heights. A few times we've felt like we needed to apologize that it wasn't as pretty as normal because of the cloud covering or simply because the mountains weren't shining as much that day. Without exception, everyone has rejected our apology with unabashed awe of what they were seeing.

As I was thinking about their reactions, I realized that I may have allowed my awe to fade. When we first moved here, I would get up every morning and look out our front window in awe at the beauty of the mountains. Now, I'm ashamed to say, I don't do that every day. I still enjoy looking at them, but they don't capture my attention like they used to.

Creation

As I sat eating lunch beside a high mountain lake, the Lord showed me how purposeful and detailed He was when creating our world. He made that lake high up in the mountains to collect the water from the winter snows and summer rains. The water is released down the creek to provide for all of the plants and animals that live along the mountain range. That water then flows down to join other creeks and rivers providing water for irrigation and us to use.

Think about the diversity of the plants and animals that are found throughout the globe. It's mind-boggling to consider. Each plant and animal is uniquely designed to live where the Lord placed it.

Marmots live at around 12,000 feet, able to thrive through the snow of winter and sun of summer. Penguins generally live by the sea near the South Pole, uniquely designed to thrive in that environment. We don't find pecan trees in the Colorado mountains nor aspens common in Texas. The animals, trees, bushes, and flowers are all designed for the conditions of their homes.

Creator

As we view the world, whether from the mountains, a lake, or the beach, we should praise the Creator. The creation is amazing. The Creator is even more incredible!

How do we describe God? Some might describe Him as a Good Father. We can use some of His attributes such as being Loving, Just, or Righteous. We can talk about the Trinity - Father, Son, and Holy Spirit. Even more than His creation, it is impossible to adequately describe the vastness, diversity, and amazing beauty of God.

I find that when attempting to describe God, I am simply reduced to amazement and awe. All I know to do then is to worship Him.

Scripture says that all of creation will worship the Lord (Psalm 145:10-12, Isaiah 44:23). Jesus was told by the Pharisees to tell the people to stop worshiping Him and His reply was that if they stopped, the rocks themselves would cry out in worship (Luke 19:40).

I think that this is a literal and figurative worship. As we marvel at the beauty of God's creation, we are inspired to give Him glory and praise. If, instead of worshiping the Creator, we bow to the creation, we are guilty of idolatry.

Are We Awed by God?

There have been many times in my life when I've had incredible encounters with my Lord; in church services, in nature, or in the privacy of my home, while reading Scripture, when praying, and while just going about my life. Each time has been powerful, impactful, and uniquely designed for me in that moment. I'm in awe that the King of kings wants to have a personal relationship with me.

I hope that the awe never fades as it seems to do with my awe of nature. I pray that I will never get to the point where I have an opportunity to worship God and instead just go on with the task of the moment. Forgive me, Lord for the many times I've done so over the years. As I journey with Him daily, I find that He is more amazing with each step and each moment. I used to think that I would eventually get to fully know Him. Now, I'm finding that the more I know, the greater desire I have to know more. And there is so much more of Him to get to know!

When we meet personally with the Lord Almighty, do we come before Him nonchalantly or with awe? Has an encounter with Him become common to the point of lacking awe? Or do we fall before Him aware of our shortcomings as did the prophet (Isaiah 6:5)? I encourage you to not lose the awe of the Lord, allowing the extraordinary to become common. He is more than worthy of our worship and desires to journey with us as we live in complete amazement of Him.

Originally posted on www.bluefirelegacy.org by Mark Henslee on 08/30/19

Live Your Life as a Conqueror!

"No, in all these things we are more than conquerors through him who loved us. For I am sure that neither death nor life, nor angels nor rulers, nor things present nor things to come, nor powers, nor height nor depth, nor anything else in all creation, will be able to separate us from the love of God in Christ Jesus our Lord." (Romans 8:37-39, ESV)

As Christians, we are told that we are more than conquerors (Romans 8:37). But how many of us live that? There seems to be a tendency to live *under* the circumstances we face instead of *above* them. We often hide from the devil's schemes instead of attacking them.

For example, we eliminate things from our lives that can be good because of a negative possibility. I was counseling with an individual who has struggled with pornography, specifically on the internet. He said that he hates smartphones because of the internet access. Since I have a smartphone, I've been thinking about if the phone is the issue or something else. I've never viewed porn on my smartphone and wouldn't know how to get to it, yet he said that it is "automatically" there. Scripture does tell us to avoid the path of the wicked (Proverbs 4:15), which means to avoid compromising situations. So, there is wisdom in putting protections in place for things such as internet porn. My concern though, is that this individual is living in fear of temptation instead of conquering it.

We are given numerous examples in Scripture of God's victory over the enemy. But do we live it in our lives? Are you known by the demons as one that is strong or weak? Does the devil want to use his limited resources against you or someone else? He's not stupid, and he seeks where he can get the best return for his efforts.

What Does it Mean for us to be Conquerors?

"Resist the devil and he will flee from you." (James 4:7, ESV) "The gates of hell shall not prevail." (Matthew 16:18, ESV) I think that to live as a conqueror is to live in the power of the Lord, defeating the enemy so that we live in the fullness of God's love.

When temptation comes, instead of being afraid, we look the enemy in the face and say, "No, in the power of the blood of Christ, I stand strong against your schemes. I command you to flee from me."

Jesus bestowed His authority to those who choose to follow Him (Matthew 28:18). This means we have the authority to stand firm against the devil - who Jesus already defeated.

How to Overcome the Schemes of the Devil

James 4:7-8, ESV says, "Submit yourselves therefore to God. Resist the devil, and he will flee from you. Draw near to God, and he will draw near to you. Cleanse your hands, you sinners, and purify your hearts, you double-minded." This Scripture is full of action that we as believers must take in order to overcome the schemes of the devil. What does it say?

We are to

- **Submit to God.** Easier said than done, but accomplished through perseverance of the faith. Submission to God is fundamental to all transformation in life (Romans 12:2). We need to be willing to say, "Not my will, but yours, be done" just as Christ did (Luke 22:42, ESV).

- **Resist, resist, resist.** Just because there is temptation doesn't mean it has the power to make you fall. You truly have the free will to resist all temptation. It is a choice to be obedient to God instead of self. We do this by choosing to cast out the thoughts and desires of the flesh (1 Corinthians 10:13). Often, we have to resist more than once. The enemy doesn't give up easily and neither should we.

- **Draw near to God.** When you feel like you successfully overcame temptation, draw near to God. More importantly, when you fail to resist, don't pull away - draw near to God! Yahweh loves and restores. He expects change from you, but He loves so deeply as to walk with you through the struggle towards the change (Jeremiah 29:12-14).

- **Cleanse our hands.** The proverbial "washing our hands" of a situation, a vice, a relationship, a selfish desire is required of us. We have to step away from the situation. Washing our hands also allows us to enter into the courts of praising our Heavenly Father - for we are called to be holy as He is holy (1 Peter 1:16).

- **Purify our hearts**. At the end of the day, God is most concerned about the state of our hearts. For such is that, "what comes out of the mouth proceeds from the heart, and this defiles a person" (Matthew 15:18, ESV). Confession of sins and turning away from them is necessary so that the enemy doesn't have things to hold against us.

Put on the Armor of God

Ephesians 6:10-11, ESV says, "Finally, be strong in the Lord and in the strength of His might. Put on the whole armor of God, that you may be able to stand against the schemes of the devil." You have the protection of the Lord in your toolbox - but are you being cognizant enough to wear the armor of the Lord daily?

We have found that, when going to battle, having the proper protective gear on is important. Battle securely in the helmet of salvation, breastplate of righteousness and belt of truth. Be ready with the gospel of peace and wield the sword of the Spirit effectively. For a more in-depth look at the armor of God check out our book *Behind Enemy Lines: A Discipleship Course in Spiritual Warfare*.

Get Close to the Father

We see in James 4 that the key to conquering sin and temptation is our *proximity* to God. James tells us to submit and draw near to God. Paul tells us to be strong in the Lord (Ephesians 6:10). We are NOT righteous enough, strong enough, pure enough, good enough, or anything else enough to stand on our own. If we attempt to go at the devil in our strength, we'll end up like the sons of Sceva (Acts 19). That's a scary thought. Understand that our victory is all about our position with the Lord.

As children, when we did things that our parents disapproved of, we knew that we couldn't go ask for favors. We would be afraid to be in their presence because of our shame. It's similar with our heavenly Father.

When we are living in sin, we are embarrassed to be seen in church; we don't spend time in prayer and worship; we don't want to be in the Father's presence. But the great thing about God is that He doesn't look at us in our sin! He sees us only through the blood of Christ. His love for us is so deep, so wide, so incredible that even when we mess everything up, He still loves us and sees us as His child. When we come to the Father with humble hearts in true repentance, He forgives and restores us to our proper place. That place is in His grace and love – in His presence.

Live As a Conqueror

If you are feeling like less than a conqueror, follow what James and Paul tell us: Submit to God; Cleanse your hands; Purify your heart; Be strong in the Lord; Put on the whole armor of God. Then you will be "more than a conqueror through him who loved us" (Romans 8:37, ESV). For nothing "will be able to separate us from the love of God in Christ Jesus our Lord" (Romans 8:39, ESV).

Originally posted on www.bluefirelegacy.org by Mark Henslee on 08/24/18

6
Edification and Exhortation

Thanksgiving Adventures and the Power of Words

"Whoever keeps his mouth and his tongue keeps himself out of trouble." (Proverbs 21:23, ESV)

Don't Do It

My brother had come to visit my parents a little before Thanksgiving, so that he could spend time with both sides of the family during the holiday. His wife had to stay home to work, and as expected, shipping schedules sometimes unexpectedly accelerate. The Christmas gift he ordered for her was going to arrive prior to his return home.

Dutifully, he warned her not to get the packages on the stoop, so as to not ruin the surprise. Then, just to be a little contrary (you'd have to meet him to fully understand), he watched on their security camera from his cell phone just in case she tried to sneak a peek.

The front door creaked, and he said over the speaker, "Don't do it." We laughed, and she complied.

Boundaries

There are some things that we just shouldn't do and certainly words that we shouldn't speak. The Lord created and communicated boundaries for us, because He knows what environments and circumstances we thrive in and those which will be more likely to create chaos and difficult hardships. While the Ten Commandments are an obvious place to start, this concept goes beyond the establishment of Law. Take every thought captive (2 Cor. 10:5), think on wholesome things (Phil. 4:8), speak life and peace (Prov. 18:21).

What Else Can Go Wrong?

While we were visiting my parents, both my brother and Mark helped my dad with various maintenance projects. The larger ones included patching a roof and dealing with a leaking toilet. The day after my brother left to go home, Mark and I discovered that the lint catching area of mom's dryer needed to be cleaned extensively. Mark pulled apart the dryer, so we could get that done.

Then, Mark was helping with cleanup from a meal and the garbage disposal started backing up. What we didn't realize is that the disposal hadn't been used in ages and was non-functional. As he scooped out all the food particles that had gone down the hatch, he was lamenting the grossness factor.

We decided to nap a bit that day, and I woke to a text from my brother asking if Mark could pick up a dishwasher and install it for mom and dad. Yep, you guessed it. The dishwasher went kaput while we were visiting. My valiant husband really despises plumbing work, but being a good son-in-law, went to work pulling out the old dishwasher and installing the new one.

Dinner was late so we opted for pizza rather than the homemade fried chicken that was on the menu for the evening. We finished eating and were cleaning up when my dad said, "I wonder what else will …." Mark immediately interrupted with, "Don't. Don't finish that statement. Don't say it."

The next day, I got up and showered. The shower backed up. The toilet that had been worked on earlier seemed to be leaking, and the other toilets were making that dreaded bubbling and gurgling sound. This isn't the first time Mark has gotten to help clean mom and dad's sewer pipes. Yep, it's Thanksgiving with a houseful of guests, and we're having extensive plumbing issues.

Words Have Power

I was sharing the conversation that my dad and Mark had the night before with my mom after we discovered the extensive nature of our circumstances. She said, "We really shouldn't say things that might give the devil ideas."

There is a spirit realm that can be influenced by our words. While I do not subscribe to the theory that we create our own reality with our words, I do believe that we can partner with the Kingdom of Light or the Kingdom of Darkness with the syllables we utter (James 3:9-12).

We can set something negative in motion with intent or naively. Anytime we agree with unholy spirits, we surrender a measure of power to them. You may experience this with fear, illness, judgment, unforgiveness, etc. It can impact you individually, as a couple/family, and even generationally.

The blessing and favor of the Lord can also be conveyed through words. Think about dry bones being called to life (Ezekiel 37:1-14). The Lord can cause us to have words of encouragement and hope for those around us that are fighting to tread emotional water. He can also cause us to see what is coming, or what an individual can grow into, even though it isn't currently in existence.

If you have the opportunity to speak judgment, condemnation, or chaos, don't do it. Instead, ask the Lord how He sees the situation and what your involvement in it is. You have the ability to change the atmosphere with the power of your words. Use them wisely.

Originally posted on www.bluefirelegacy.org by Dallas Henslee on 12/08/19

Building Beautiful Sandcastles in the Church

"And the rain fell, and the floods came, and the winds blew and beat on that house, but it did not fall, because it had been founded on the rock." (Matthew 7:25, ESV)

During a recent time away from the ministry, we were able to enjoy time on the beach. The water was a little too cold to enjoy, so many families opted to play in the sand rather than the water. We saw one or two elaborate, and some not so elaborate, sandcastles.

I usually read Christian fiction when we are on vacation. This excursion was no different. and the book's author used pastoral family dynamics as a portion of the storyline. Together, the visual sand edifices and the book made me think about all the work to erect something so temporary. Then, because it's an occupational hazard, I started thinking about how that applies to what we often do in our churches.

We often find ourselves discussing topics with clients that could fit into this category. It is something we are very familiar with; both from the vantage point of falling prey to the temptation to erect them and from the perspective of having them completely dismantled.

Growing Up in the Church

I was introduced to the ministry as a child. My mom tells a story about the time I crawled up into his lap and asked Dr. Beard if I could attend "big church" at the very mature age of *three*. Evidently, the nursery bored me. Pastor John said I could, but that I was expected to listen just like the grown-ups; no coloring, no playing games, no talking or whispering during service, but being fully engaged in the music and the sermon, no matter how long he was preaching that particular week. He was known to be long-winded among the adults.

I wasn't much older than that when I sang my first solo in church. Yes, I can remember the words to that little song even now. My dad entered seminary when I was 8, and we moved to Canada for him to pastor a church there. We moved while I was in the middle of fifth grade (grade five for my Canadian friends). This experience provides me a perspective of evaluating ministry from the eyes of a child, and as an adult, which assists greatly in our scope of ministry.

Priorities

As ministers, there is an innate desire to help people. The problem is, we can start to build "sandcastles" with our skewed priorities. This often happens because the minister is attempting to fulfill all the expectations, whether disclosed or presumed, reasonable or unreasonable, of congregants, parishioners, and denominational leaders.

A pastor will never be able to keep all the people happy, and to attempt to do so is simply to build a temporary castle that will all too easily be washed away. Then the pastor often begins to build another structure in the same spot on the proverbial beach to "reconcile" with those in the church who were disappointed in some way.

While individuals encountered day to day often have the loudest voices and express displeasure through complaint, it is God's opinion that is of the utmost importance. He established relationship, and He establishes priority within differing relationships. The Ten Commandments clearly express God's position. "You shall have no other gods above Me" (Exodus 20:3, ESV). That means our first ministry is to God, Himself.

As we teach priorities, God is at the top of the list, then our spouse, followed by our children and immediate family. Then all other relationships or responsibilities, including our paid ministry positions, can vie for priority depending on the season and urgency.

Organization and Numbers

Churches can be tempted to build sandcastles in leadership ranks and organization. Ministries have legal guidelines and budget considerations; however, the administration of churches and service ministries should not be approached the same way as it is by those in the business world. Churches are to be focused on spreading the gospel and dependent on God. Often, God will ask sold out Christians to do things that do not make sense through an earthly lens.

Worldly success and financial prowess do not impress the lost who are looking for the Church to be different. They may complain about our values, but they expect our values, and the expression of them in daily living, to be counter cultural. Otherwise, we are offering nothing different than anyone else and our salt has lost its usefulness (see Matthew 5:13-16).

While focusing on finances is a temporary edifice, so is a focus on numbers. Numbers are deceiving. Numbers can be manipulated, and the enemy of the saints does just that. He causes doubt in the mind of the missionary that isn't seeing tangible spiritual fruit even though they continue to faithfully labor in the field. He maliciously whispers to the pastor that is shepherding a small home church, "Surely, the impact is not sufficient to be significant to God." Conversely, he causes the leader with great charisma that can draw multitudes to be puffed up. Racking up and counting numbers is often equivalent to using seashells to decorate our castle.

The Solid Rock

Jesus taught us to build upon the Solid Rock with Him as our foundation. All of us are in need of a Savior because we are fallen and fallible. We used to sing a song in Sunday School about the foolish man and the wise man. It was always a favorite because of the accompanying hand motions. The foolish man built his house upon the sand, but the wise man built his house upon the Rock (see Matthew 7:24-27). This principle holds for both individuals and the church, made up corporately of individuals. Be sure your foundation is Christ and stands firm lest your house is built on sand and comes tumbling down.

Originally posted on www.bluefirelegacy.org by Dallas Henslee on 02/06/21

Using Our Brains in a World of Information and Technology

"All Scripture is breathed out by God and profitable for teaching, for reproof, for correction, and for training in righteousness, that the man of God may be complete, equipped for every good work." (2 Timothy 3:16-17, ESV)

There is some truth to the saying, "Use it or lose it." Mostly, I've thought of this in terms of skills and muscles, but it also applies to our brains. The brain is much like our muscles, the more we use it, the stronger and more capable it becomes.

I was recently asked by someone that has never lived without the internet, if I thought it was overall good or a detriment to our lives. In the moment, I provided some observations of things that I feel the internet has provided and things that we are missing because of the prevalence of technology in our lives. With additional time to process the question, I can identify many things that we are lacking because of our dependence upon technology.

Thinking Required

The biggest negative I have seen with technology is that we tend to stop thinking for ourselves. We have volumes of information at our fingertips, and the ability to do so much more in less time and with less effort than in the past. Yet, we allow the technology to do our thinking. There's a pandemic of lack of thought.

With the availability of calculators, it was no longer necessary to learn how to do even simple math in our heads. Ever had an experience with a cashier who couldn't figure out how much change to give back without the computer telling them?

As we have become dependent upon GPS units, and now maps on our phones, we no longer seem to know how to read a map or follow directions. This can be a real problem in rural areas like where we live, as the GPS map may not actually direct us where we want to go. For example, if you put in the address for Legacy Heights, you will get close, but you'll be about a half mile away from the driveway.

Brain Exercise

The more we exercise our brains, the stronger they become. This requires that we are constantly learning new information, and that we are processing the information, not just absorbing it.

If I push a weight on a cart across the floor, I've moved the weight and, maybe, used a few muscles. If instead, I pick up the weight and carry it to the new location, I have used more muscles. As we use our brains to wrestle with thoughts and ideas, we are building the muscles of thought.

There are many things that seem reasonable, until we think deeply about it. The surface can be deceiving. We need to be willing to wrestle with the concepts and draw meaningful conclusions, even when they are contrary to our desired outcome. The truth is not dependent upon our whims and wishes.

This applies not only to what we read and hear on the internet, it applies to what we hear from the pulpit. I'll admit that there are times when I'm preaching that my mouth doesn't say what my brain is thinking. Therefore, I have learned to give grace for the occasional misstatement. Unfortunately, there are many things being purposely taught in the name of God that are contrary to His Truth. We need to take all teaching to the Holy Spirit and the Holy Bible to determine what is beneficial to be ingested, and what is fat or bone to be discarded.

"All Scripture is breathed out by God and profitable for teaching, for reproof, for correction, and for training in righteousness, that the man of God may be complete, equipped for every good work." (2 Timothy 3:16-17, ESV)

History is Important

With all of the new information that we have available to read, I see many failing to learn from the past. When was the last time that you read something written more than 50 years ago? There is so much that we can learn from those who have lived before us. Just because we have more information does not mean that we have more wisdom.

The nature of man hasn't really changed over the centuries and millennia. When I read books written many years ago, there are commonalities that I see in our world today. There are also many lessons for us to learn of things that are good, as well as things not to repeat.

There's another saying, "Those who ignore history are bound to repeat it." I'd add that those who distort history are deceived into thinking they can avoid it. We need to understand the reality of the past, no matter how ugly, in order to learn how to live the present better.

A Measuring Rod

With the flood of information, we have to be able to decipher what is fact and what is opinion. Back in the 1980s, situational ethics popped up in the schools. I believe that this has contributed to the collapse in our nation's moral compass. We need to have a fixed standard against which to measure things. For me the Word of God (The Holy Bible) is my measuring stick for determining what is right and wrong.

Regardless of the situation, there is truth; unchanging, independent of opinion, real truth. The sun does not rise and go down based on our wishes. It is a fixed truth that only God, the Creator, can change. I can call myself whatever gender I choose, but the truth is that I have body parts specific to the male gender. I can call good evil, and evil good, but it is still either good or evil when measured against the Truth.

"We are from God, and whoever knows God listens to us; but whoever is not from God does not listen to us. This is how we recognize the Spirit of truth and the spirit of falsehood." (1 John 4:6, NIV)

Feed Your Brain

One final saying important in our discussion of the brain is, "Garbage in, garbage out." What we put into our brain is of utmost importance if we want it to be healthy and produce positive outflows.

Chemicals that we physically ingest have an impact on our brain's ability to process information. A steady stream of junk food will negatively impact our brain. I'm no expert in dietary anything, but I know from experience that my ability to think varies based on the quality of the food I eat.

The things that we read, watch, and listen to also impact our brain and especially affect our behaviors. A steady diet of shows that contain profanity will lead to the speaking of profane things. Constantly viewing negative concepts will lead to negative thought patterns that flow out in all areas of our life. Music has a powerful effect on our thoughts and emotions, for either good or bad.

While it is impossible to avoid all bad things, we need to be purposeful in what we put into our brains. We need to think about what we hear, not just accept everything at face value. God's standards do not change, so we can stand firm on His Truth, regardless of what the world is choosing to believe. With the help of the Holy Spirit, we are able to align our thoughts with the Truth in Christ.

"So Jesus said to the Jews who had believed him, 'If you abide in my word, you are truly my disciples, and you will know the truth, and the truth will set you free.'" (John 8:31-32, ESV)

Originally posted on www.bluefirelegacy.org by Mark Henslee on 04/02/21

Joined in the Fire or Cooling on the Side

"And let us consider how to stir up one another to love and good works, not neglecting to meet together, as is the habit of some, but encouraging one another, and all the more as you see the Day drawing near."

(Hebrews 10:24-25, ESV)

While watching a fire burn in our fireplace, I noticed a chunk of wood that fell to the side. It was burning bright and hot when it was in the midst of the fire, but once it fell to the side, it was not long before the flames subsided. In a relatively short time, the once hot burning piece of wood was smoldering with no flames and little heat being generated from it.

I'm like that piece of wood. When I'm in the midst of other believers who are on fire for the things of God, I tend to be fired up, so to speak. When I fall to the side, my flame has a tendency to decrease, and I become cold and non-beneficial to the world around me.

Whether we like to admit it or not, we need each other. We need to live connected with other followers of Christ. It is essential to our spiritual health. We need times of corporate worship and times of small group discussions. Hearing the

Word taught, studying it individually, and studying with a few others are of great value. There is immeasurable richness in having a close friend that holds us accountable and encourages us in our faith.

Doing Life Together

Over 20 years ago, we were a part of a small group that came together in a very special way. We truly lived life together. This group was even responsible for helping to name one of our daughters. More than two decades later, we can get together with others from the group and feel as if hardly any time has passed at all. The spiritual bond that was formed in those meetings continues today.

Not all small groups get to that level of connection, but that doesn't mean that we shouldn't strive for it. In a small group setting, we are able to be more connected than in a large corporate gathering. We are able to care for each other in the daily reality of life.

If you are not already a part of a small group of believers that meets together regularly, I encourage you to find a group. It doesn't have to be tied to a single church but can be a blend of people from your community. Yes, it may involve a risk to join, but it is well worth it when you experience the depth of connection possible.

Going Bigger

There are different levels of togetherness. I love small groups. There is an intimacy and level of care that isn't present in large gatherings. But we also need to have regular times of gathering with larger groups of Christians.

While the work of the ministry has us in a variety of churches throughout the year, we have a home church. A place where we are known and know others. A place where we are a part of the body and able to contribute as well as receive encouragement. It's not a perfect church (it has people in it after all), but it is an important part of our spiritual life.

Regardless of the style of worship gathering, there is energy and power when we gather in large groups. Singing, corporately reading scripture, and reciting liturgy together in one accord is powerful. Remembering the Lord's sacrifice for us by sharing communion with others has value in our spirits as we are joined with Him and His bride, the Church.

We are also able to serve the Body of Christ by being a member of a local church body. As Paul tells us in 1 Corinthians 12, we are all members of one body with different roles and talents. The Body needs every one of us to be complete. When a Christian decides to go through life apart from the Church, not only do they miss out, but the whole body suffers for lack of being complete with all of its members.

Being a part of a local church is not as much about you as it is about the Body. Instead of asking what the church can offer you, ask what you can offer the church. How can you serve the Lord by serving the church?

Time Set Apart

Each of us has different levels of need for being with others and being alone. Also, *how* we spend our time alone will vary so it is important for me not to impose on you my style and *vice versa*. God walks with us in the still and quiet, as well as in the busy and chaotic. We need to be purposeful in spending time with Him apart from others without neglecting the gathering together with other believers.

It's not uncommon for me to unwind by sitting and staring at a burning fire. I also need time to wander in nature with my dog. These times of being apart from others and removed from the chaos of life are vital to my emotional and spiritual health. I often get to hear truths from the Lord in the process.

I also need another man that knows me deeply and has permission to speak into my life. It may be more formal as accountability partners or just a friend that is closer than a brother. There is greater vulnerability and ability to grow when I walk in a relationship with another in this manner.

Jump in the Fire

Living the Christian life is fullest when we live it with others. When joined in the fire with other believers, we will be stronger, and we will burn brighter for the world to see.

I encourage all believers to have a close friend that has permission to call them to accountability, to be a part of a small group of believers that live life together, and to be active members of a local church where they can worship corporately, as well as serve the Body of Christ. It's not about one or the other, it's best when we have all of the methods of togetherness.

Originally posted on www.bluefirelegacy.org by Mark Henslee on 02/21/20

7

Community and Unity

Slipping on the Hills of Life

"The steps of a man are established by the Lord, when he delights in his way; though he fall, he shall not be cast headlong, for the Lord upholds his hand."

(Psalms 37:23-24, ESV)

Living in Colorado, we get snow. Generally, I don't have issues with driving on snow, but the other day, that was not the case. Our car was in need of new tires, and I had been putting it off for financial reasons. Well, that ended up not being a good decision.

I had gone to the ministry property, and while attempting to go up the drive, I was unable to get all the way up. When backing down the narrow, snow covered, slick drive with inadequate tread on the tires, I went off the side and into a tree. With one tire suspended in the air and the side of the car implanted in the midst of tree branches, I was stuck.

Asking for Help

After crying out to God that this was not in my plans for the day, I had to come up with a way to get the car out. Dallas was at home and could have brought our other vehicle, but it likely wouldn't be big enough to pull the Acadia out of its predicament. So, a little hiking was necessary.

I walked the roughly half mile to the neighbors and humbly knocked on the door to see if he could help. (For those of you who read my blogs regularly, you are familiar with my humility lessons.) Fortunately, the neighbor was home and willing to help.

Enough Power to Pull

The neighbor brought his little tractor up with the thought it would be sufficient to pull the car out. After trying a few different angles, it was obvious that the tractor wasn't enough. We needed something heavier, with more power. Time for plan B. He drove the tractor back home and brought his pickup truck.

It required some effort, but with enough weight and power pulling, we were able to get the Acadia back on the driveway. Unfortunately, that wasn't all that was needed. The tree branches tore off the passenger side mirror. And, in the process of sliding, I managed to slice one of the tires. I backed the car down to a relatively flat part of the drive and changed the tire for the spare.

An Acadia isn't a small vehicle, nor is it a large SUV like a Suburban, but it is big enough that one of those Mickey Mouse spares just drives weird. (Especially on snow covered, dirt roads.) Alas, I was able to slowly drive home. A couple hours later than planned.

Get a Grip

As I was hiking back from the neighbor's, a little calmer than on the walk down, I knew that there was a lesson in this adventure. At the time, it wasn't very clear. The next day, when telling a friend about the event, it became obvious.

In our spiritual lives, just like when driving, we need to have good traction.

Regardless of the length, and breadth, of our journey with the Lord, we will have times of difficulty. These may look like hills to go up, where, without the right amount of grip, you aren't going to make it. Maybe it is an unexpected slick spot, like an ice patch or snow on the road. In our journeys, these may look like temptations or difficult people. It may be somewhere that you have been a hundred times before, but this time it's different. Whatever it is that comes your way, do you have enough tread?

When we don't keep ourselves properly "treaded", trouble and damage may result. In the case of our car, it was a sliced tire, a broken mirror, dents and scratches along the side. In our spiritual journey, the damage could be to relationships, peace of mind, or comfort; or there may be any number of other problems that arise from our slipping.

How do you make sure that you have adequate spiritual tread? It all depends on our connection with the Lord. **Jesus and the Holy Spirit are our tread.** When we have Him as our connection to the things of this world, we can maintain traction. In His love and with the fruit of the Spirit, we are able to safely navigate the hard days of life.

Damage Repair

After the accident, I had to assess the damage and go about making repairs. New tires were purchased, a new mirror and matching paint were ordered. The scratches will remain as a reminder for the future of things to avoid (and of my gratitude for Dallas being a forgiving wife since the Acadia is primarily her vehicle).

When we get off the path in our life journey, we need to assess the damage and make repairs just like with the car. There will often be a cost involved. Despite how much you may try, sheer force of willpower will not correct the damage and make it all go away. You must make time and space for repairing the damage in your life.

What repairs are needed, and how we go about them, will depend on the damage done. Often, this requires going to other people to apologize and seek restoration of relationships. In all situations, we need to go to our Heavenly Father and ask forgiveness, which He promises to grant (1 John 1:9).

Some scars may remain as reminders for us in the future. We all have baggage from our past (and sometimes our present). It is easy to beat ourselves up for years. That is not a healthy response. Instead, when we receive God's forgiveness, we need to also forgive ourselves. We need to use the lessons of the past for a healthy walk in the future. If you're unsure about *how* to forgive, we provide practical tools in our forgiveness book, *Breaking the Burdensome Yoke*.

For about a week, while waiting for the part, we drove with a broken mirror. It made lane changes a bit interesting, but there was enough there to still see and drive safely. Mirrors on the car allow us to see what is behind and beside us. It is important to remember the past and be looking around, but our focus needs to be on what is ahead.

How's Your Traction?

When you look at your spiritual life, are you "treaded" in Jesus? Do you have a good connection with the Lord, and are you walking continually in communion with Him? It is vital that we spend quality time in Scripture, prayer and worship. It is also essential that we have Godly accountability in people that journey with us.

We all have our moments when we slip. When you slip, make the repairs necessary to move forward well. As you grow and mature, those times should become less frequent. Don't allow mistakes to define who you are and inhibit you from doing the things that the Lord has called you to do.

Originally posted on www.bluefirelegacy.org by Mark Henslee on 12/14/18

Living in the Desert

"Therefore encourage one another and build one another up, just as you are doing. We ask you, brothers, to respect those who labor among you and are over you in the Lord and admonish you, and to esteem them very highly in love because of their work. Be at peace among yourselves. And we urge you, brothers, admonish the idle, encourage the fainthearted, help the weak, be patient with them all."

(1 Thessalonians 5:11-14, ESV)

Recently, someone told us that we were rubbing off on them. This individual continued by saying, "I dreamed we were going to sell everything and move into a house in the desert." Initially, I discounted this statement as simply processing our visit the night before, but I have come to believe it carries much more weight. That suspicion was validated when another friend offered the same insight into this particular piece of the story.

The house in the desert is where Mark and I currently are; literally and figuratively. This thought had already occurred to me before my friend's validating comment, however, what she said next was a new thought that I needed to unpack. So, settle in as we look at her observation, "Good things happen in the desert."

Good Things in the Desert

Deserts are reported to cover a third of the earth, and they don't have to be hot to qualify for the designation. They can be cold - think Antarctica; and beautiful - think Colorado. To qualify as a desert, though, there must be a lack of moisture. However, a lack does not mean an absence.

It is possible to sustain life in the desert. While water is sparse, the soil is rich with nutrients for growth. Deserts have plant and animal inhabitants that have adapted to the harsh conditions. They know how to use the water efficiently and how to mitigate the detrimental effects of heat.

When I think about stories from the Bible that involve the desert, I tend to jump to the wandering for forty years aspect. That is a long time to be in the desert. However, when we look past the time frame, there were a lot of other things happening. In addition to experiencing a consequence for disobedience, the Israelites were being taught and restored to God. Their shoes didn't wear out. Their clothes didn't disintegrate. They had food and obviously enough water to survive. They learned dependence on their Creator rather than self-reliance.

When I apply some of these observations personally, I realize that God is teaching and preparing me. I am having to depend on God for sustenance and sufficient water for my body, soul, and spirit. In the absence of abundance, I have to learn how to find the water and use it efficiently.

Rationing Water

In the natural, it becomes necessary at times to ration water. Similarly, it may become necessary to tuck away special times of corporate worship and biblical teaching to sustain you through times that you are not in your normal routine, a time when an unforeseen crisis has hit, or you are operating for the time right at the edge of your healthy boundaries. Familiar Scriptures and hymns or praise songs often come to mind for me during such times. Fortunately, Jesus said He is the Living Water and that Source never runs dry.

There is a depth of connection to that Living Water that sustains one even when living in the desert. That depth provides assurance of survival without a constant need for light soaking rains. Yes, these times are refreshing, but dependance on constant light rains does not develop deep roots.

Sharing Your Water

One of the ways animals can survive in the desert is to eat from plants that store water. There are times when you may be the one that is planted and providing water to those around you. Other times, you may be the one in search of life sustaining plants. Think about the biblical mandates of living in community and mentoring/discipling. We can see some of the instructions in these passages:

Psalm 133:1 It is good for God's people to live in unity

Matthew 28:19-20 Go to the nations baptizing and teaching believers

Acts 2:46-47 They worshiped, ate, and enjoyed favor with each other

Romans 12:4-5, 16 The body needs each of its parts; live in peace with each other

Colossians 3:16 Teach and encourage each other with Godly principles

2 Timothy 4:1-2 Preach the Word in season and out, correct, rebuke, encourage

Hebrews 10:24-25 Continue to meet together, encouraging each other in love and good deeds

When God designed the ecosystem of the desert, He created plants that could withstand the elements in addition to sustaining other life. Are you looking for water or sharing your water? Regardless of which category you currently fall into, I would implore you to evaluate how you are going about it.

Refreshing Living Water

Each of our desert experiences are likely different, but God is great at preparing us, and meeting us, in our desert times. Know that you are not alone even when it seems you cannot turn to those around you for encouragement and support. God is there, and He has designed a way to sustain you.

How are you learning to depend on your Creator rather than indulging in self-reliance? What are some of the ways He is providing for you despite your immediate circumstances or environment? How are you helping others in the desert? Where do you find The Living Water and get refreshed by Him?

You may be in a desert, but remember, good things happen in the desert.

Originally posted on www.bluefirelegacy.org by Dallas Henslee on 01/04/19

Parenting Truths You Can Use in Any Relationship

"So I exhort the elders among you, as a fellow elder and a witness of the sufferings of Christ, as well as a partaker in the glory that is going to be revealed: shepherd the flock of God that is among you, exercising oversight, not under compulsion, but willingly, as God would have you; not for shameful gain, but eagerly; not domineering over those in your charge, but being examples to the flock."

(1 Peter 5:1-3, ESV)

We recently celebrated Mother's Day and Father's Day so I've been thinking about parenting. My kids are now adults living independent lives, and yet, I'm still working on figuring out how to parent well. I've asked many people through the years how to handle various situations and be the best dad I can possibly be. There's been plenty of good, helpful advice, as well as a significant number of suggestions that weren't so good.

Through it all, I've learned a few truths. These are written from a parenting perspective; however, I believe you can apply them to just about any relationship.

Pray Continually

Pray for your kids; whether they've yet to be conceived, are driving you nuts as preschoolers, in the midst of elementary school, teenagers or adults. Petition the Lord for protection, health, and guidance. Pray for their spouses-to-be or those that are now part of your family.

Prayer is simply talking with God. We generally are fairly good at asking for the things that we want. We also need to be good at listening to His input. It's a two-way conversation. As I grow, I'm discovering that I need to be listening more than talking in my conversations, especially with the Lord.

Pray for wisdom and understanding. We need the Lord's wisdom more than another self-help book on parenting. No one knows your kids and what they need more than God, so we might as well ask the expert to reveal how best to understand them.

Without the help and intervention of the Holy Spirit, it is impossible to achieve much. I've made so many mistakes as a parent that I'm amazed at how the Lord has overcome my shortcomings with His incredible grace and mercy.

Love Unconditionally

Your kids are not perfect, and yet, they still need your love in the midst of everything. They need to be celebrated when they do good. They need to be disciplined *in love* when they mess up, held when they are hurting, and loved regardless of their performance.

I have to admit that there are days that I don't like my kids very much. It's just not possible to always like someone. Heck, some days I don't even like myself much. But regardless of how much I like, or temporarily dislike them, I hope they know that I love them. There is absolutely nothing that my kids can do to lose my love for them.

Unconditional love is more powerful than all of the forces of the enemy. Love is a primary characteristic of God (see 1 John 4), and when we operate in love, we are emulating our Heavenly Father.

Model Honestly

There is so much more caught than taught. "Do what I say, not what I do" just doesn't work. Kids are watching everything that you do, and they will believe your actions far more than your words.

This is especially true with how you handle yourself when you make a mistake. If you expect your kids to be humble and apologetic when in the wrong, then you should model that yourself. Show them how to own their stuff by taking responsibility for your actions.

I've met far too many parents who seem to think that they can't let their kids know that they aren't perfect. I hate to break it to you, but the kids already know it, so you might as well talk about it with them. How else are they going to learn how to recover from a fall?

Model forgiveness, humility, grace, and mercy. Model how to journey with God in the good times and the hard times. Show your kids, through your actions, how to be a Christ-follower by modeling the fruit of the Spirit (see Galatians 5:22-23).

Talk Openly

Open communication will overcome so many shortfalls. When we don't have open and honest conversations, then assumptions are made on one or both sides of the table. Assumptions are rarely beneficial and most often have some degree of error in them.

Talk about the good stuff *and* the hard stuff. Some conversations are difficult, but we need to have them even if they are uncomfortable. Don't dance around the elephant in the room, address it. Share your life and ask about their life.

Be available when they need you. If you say, "In a minute," be sure that it is only a minute. By being there and listening, they will feel valued and more likely to come to you with things in the future. Listen attentively, not just to the words but to the meaning behind what is being said.

We also need to be talking about God in everyday situations. Don't limit Him to church or a short prayer before meals. Talk about His creation as you walk together. Tell your kids the stories of the Lord working in your life. Literally apply Deuteronomy 6:7 to your family life, as well as all your other relationships.

Treat Uniquely

Every person is unique, not just our fingerprints and DNA, but our personalities, emotions, and dreams. There is not a one-size-fits-all approach to parenting. Learn about who your child is, and respond accordingly.

Each of my kids is unique, even my twins who might look alike are very different people. We need to celebrate each child's uniqueness. Discipline in a manner that they can receive the correction. Learn their love language, and learn how to speak it with them. Discover who they are, and custom tailor your parenting to each one.

One of my favorite things in the work that we do is to see God meet with each person uniquely. When coming alongside ministers and their families, we have seen so many different ways that the Lord interacts with each person. For example, I have an exercise that I use to deal with shame. The process is fairly simple, the result is the same goal of freedom, and yet the individual experiences are so incredibly different.

Walk Out the Truths

As we all walk in relationship with people, especially with our kids, we will face difficulties, experience joys and heartaches, make mistakes, and get a few things right. Applying these truths will help us to have healthier, fulfilling relationships.

How can you apply these truths to your relationships? Do you pray regularly for your kids, family, friends, co-workers? Are you loving the people in your life unconditionally? Do you model being a Christ follower? Are you talking openly about life in a way that people see God? Do you treat each person that you interact with uniquely as God created them?

Originally posted on www.bluefirelegacy.org by Mark Henslee on 07/10/20

Unity Through the Strength of Diversity

"I in them and you in me, that they may become perfectly one, so that the world may know that you sent me and loved them even as you loved me." (John 17:23)

We recently had the privilege of visiting Chicago, IL for the first time. Many things can be said about Chicago; the food, the architecture; the weather; the traffic; the people. There is a great amount of diversity in seemingly everything. Just about every culture and people group are represented in the city and surrounding area.

Seeing the great diversity in one area has me thinking about the Church. As we work around the world, we get to see the Body of Christ in its many variations of culture, styles, personalities, and theologies. I sense that most Americans think that the Church looks and acts like them, or at least should. The reality is that we can be united in Christ while celebrating our differences.

A Diverse Group

One day, the Church (big C meaning the global Church), will be made up of people from every tribe and tongue (Revelation

7:9). What an incredible gathering that will be when we get to see the Lord high and lifted up, and the greatness of His creativity in creating such a diverse group of people.

God made every one of us unique. We have some commonalities with others, but in total, we are who we are, and no one else is exactly like us. Therefore, we should not expect everyone to act, believe, or think as we do.

The Body of Christ includes not just a variety of skin colors and languages, we also have a diversity of practices. The key is that we all believe that Jesus Christ is the one and only way to eternity with the Father in Heaven. When we agree on Christ, we can then agree to disagree on the minor things.

Take, for example, the style of worship. We recently visited a church that had a worship experience that is different from my preferred way of worshiping. While I was not fully engaged because of the style, there were many people who were fully encountering the Lord in that service. In all likelihood, they would struggle in a service that fits my preferences. Neither is wrong; they're just different.

Strength in Diversity

Too often, we see these differences as reasons to separate from others. Sometimes, we will even declare that another group is not Christian because of the differences. We need to be diligent in practicing sound doctrine, but I dare say too often, some cry, "heresy" when it really is just an alternate interpretation or preference.

An astronaut is able to give perspective and insight to someone who believes the earth is flat. The flat-earther may not be convinced that the world is round, but I'm sure that they will not convince the astronaut that it is flat. There is absolute truth, and we can find it in Scripture with the help of the Holy Spirit. There are also different perspectives and interpretations of positions. Some things we will not fully know until we are in eternity with the Lord.

What I have found is that when I engage with other believers of different streams, I am challenged to go deeper in my relationship with the Lord. They encourage me to see beyond my current understanding. That doesn't mean that I change my beliefs or practices, but it challenges me to see God as bigger than I had previously seen Him, and hopefully, to know Him better.

I encourage believers to get outside of their circle; to meet with believers from other denominations, and read books by people that you may not agree with. Don't adopt everything that you read or hear without testing it, including from your home church. Too often, we value the sayings of men more than going to the source of Truth. We need to test everything through the Holy Spirit and His Word, the Holy Bible (See 1 John 4:1-6).

Discomfort is Expected

As we step outside of our circle, we should expect it to be uncomfortable. We may hear or see things that don't fit our preconceived notions of how God works. Some of it will be of man, and therefore, not of God. Other things may be the Lord wanting to teach you more about Himself. The problem with shutting out everything we are uncomfortable with is that we will likely miss the things God wants to show us.

Jesus didn't make life comfortable for His disciples when He walked the earth. We shouldn't expect to be comfortable either. Get out of your comfort zone. There is strength to be gained when we walk through the discomfort.

Seek opportunities to be stretched in your faith. Ask the Lord to show you aspects of Himself that you haven't seen before. He is so much bigger than we will ever comprehend or even be able to wrap our head around. And when He shows you more of Himself, embrace it.

Together in Unity

Dallas and I are very different people, and yet, we are united as a couple. Our marriage would be quite boring if we were exactly alike. She has strengths where I am weak, and vice versa. Together, we are more than the sum of the parts.

Similarly, Christians are different in many ways. When we join together in Christ, we can do more than when we remain separated. One may bring a deeper knowledge of Scripture and another a broader experience of the Holy Spirit. Together, we can know and experience the fullness of God. This is true individually and corporately working together as various church bodies to impact our local communities.

When we know the Truth, we are able to be free from the bonds of judgment and separation from other believers. Jesus prayed in John 17 that all believers would live in unity. We can unite around Jesus Christ, even as we maintain our diversity.

When we see our differences as strengths, we can come together in unity for the purpose of sharing the Gospel of Jesus Christ to all people. Our love for one another should outweigh all of our preferences. Together in Christ, we can be one.

Originally posted on www.bluefirelegacy.org by Mark Henslee on 10/30/20

8
Rest and Restoration

Are You Pouring From a Broken Carafe?

"But He would withdraw to desolate places and pray."
(Luke 5:16, ESV)

It wasn't a great way to start the work week. I went to retrieve the coffee carafe from the dishwasher only to find the glass had broken. The placement of the break wouldn't have negatively impacted the ability of the carafe to hold the volume of desired liquid. The concern, however, was the potential negative effect of the application of additional heat. Pouring out of the coffee pot without causing harm, due to misdirected and unrestrained leakage was also a slight gamble.

It had been a busy weekend with additional travel, so not having coffee wasn't even a momentary consideration. I pulled out my percolator that I have as a backup to use on the gas range if the power goes out. I'm not as familiar with this alternate prep method, and I let it perk too long. I normally drink my coffee black, but this cup was a TAD strong. I deemed it consumable with a little fixing up, so cream and hot chocolate powder were added making a lovely "in a pinch" mocha *sans* whipped cream on top.

Unrealistic Expectations and Burnout

As I pondered the events, there seemed to be a spiritual application. It dawned on me, post coffee consumption, that this is a picture of how Christians, can impact the world around them. Unfortunately, sometimes we still try to do all the things we've done before, even though we are broken. Especially for those serving in leadership roles in churches or other ministries, there is an illusion that we have enough capacity to just keep going. I'm not really sure where this line of thought took root, but it is nefarious. Not only is it an outrageous and unrealistic expectation, it can create long-term consequences leading to burn-out or even an exit, whether forced or voluntary, from ministry altogether.

In contrast to the damaging thought pattern, I can point to numerous passages where Jesus found it necessary to pull away and refresh. He modeled **not** being *"on"* all the time. He did what He saw His Father doing (Genesis 2:2; John 5:19-20). God the Father modeled and prescribed rest. He did so because of our need for rest.

Rest is Modeled and Prescribed

In our ministry at Blue Fire Legacy, we frequently teach on taking a Sabbath or longer times of rest. Sometimes, it is necessary to look at what sabbaticals are, and what they are not, with clients. Pushing ourselves past the point of our natural limitations is damaging for us *and* those around us. Mark and I teach on these subjects because we have experienced the fatigue of overextending and living in opposition to God's instructions. We can fall into this trap because we are attempting to meet the expectations of various individuals, or out of a desire to receive accolades, recognition, and/or the praise of man. We've been there, but we've also learned how to minister from a place of rest.

Remember the coffee pot? It's been around a long time. All the pulling out and pushing back in probably created a stress fracture that the heat and pressure of the dishwasher exploited.

We can experience the same phenomenon. If we're overly pressed for time to complete routine tasks and stressed, the next heat point (conflict or difference of opinion) or pressure (demands or expectations to get one more thing done) can cause us to break. In those moments, we are usually unable to refrain from speaking or acting harshly towards another.

Even if we pull ourselves back together, somewhat, there is still a noticeable chip or break point. It is important to pull away for a time, check our heart condition, and be healed or restored by the Lord before coming back into a place of service on a larger scale. If we remain in service while damaged, we may unintentionally cut or burn someone around us as we pour out.

Solitude and Prayer

Jesus pulled away to find solitude and pray. In some translations, Luke 5:16 includes the word "frequently" or "often". This indicates it was not a sporadic or exceptional event. Let's look at this in context.

> "While Jesus was in one of the towns, a man came along who was covered with leprosy. When he saw

Jesus, he fell with his face to the ground and begged him, "Lord, if you are willing, you can make me clean."

Jesus reached out his hand and touched the man. "I am willing," he said. "Be clean!" And immediately the leprosy left him.

Then Jesus ordered him, "Don't tell anyone, but go, show yourself to the priest and offer the sacrifices that Moses commanded for your cleansing, as a testimony to them."

Yet the news about him spread all the more, so that crowds of people came to hear him and to be healed of their sicknesses. But Jesus often withdrew to lonely places and prayed." (Luke 5:12-16, NIV)

Jesus pulled away as a regular practice even while engaging in active ministry. Living life and ministering from a place of rest, permits better results than running ourselves into the ground in an attempt to *earn* a time of rest. I encourage you to look at how you approach ministry and life, and make the necessary changes so that you can operate out of rest in Him. It's okay to stop pouring out of the broken carafe for a time of rest and healing with the Lord.

Originally posted on www.bluefirelegacy.org by Dallas Henslee on 07/16/21

Restlessness in the Face of Rest

"And he said to them, "Come away by yourselves to a desolate place and rest a while." For many were coming and going, and they had no leisure even to eat. And they went away in the boat to a desolate place by themselves." (Mark 6:31-32, ESV)

We talk to a lot of church leaders about rest and creating healthy boundaries. I read an article recently that said when the hours church members expected their pastors to be spending in various job-related activities were summed, the expectations added up to over 100 hours a week.

Church leaders and support staff are not the only ones susceptible to packed schedules. As a culture, our schedules have grown so busy that we dream about vacations and retirement because of the promise of rest. There are even studies showing that vacations can have a positive impact on work efficacy and production. However, God modeled more frequent rest periods than once a year, or after a celebrated career concludes.

He rested after creating the universe complete with time, land, water, plants, animals, and mankind. He instructed us to observe a Sabbath, and He appointed festivals; another way of refocusing and laying aside day-to-day life to be renewed.

When Mark was running his own public accounting practice, and we were involved in bi-vocational ministry, we would find it necessary to leave for a time of vacation and renewal at the beach after the conclusion of tax season. We discovered that it took us a few days to unwind and let go of the "normal" pace and simply *be still*. We also have made a distinction between types of travel, dividing it into two categories: trips and vacations. Trips typically involve a schedule and meeting with various people or attending conferences. Vacations on the other hand, allow us to simply *be* and occur in places of nature that are restorative to us.

The Problem

The problem is that some of us have forgotten how to rest or have figured out a way to warp play into something with productive value, thereby turning it into work. We, as a collective culture, have come to believe, erroneously, that the harder we work, the more valuable we are. We have been duped into believing that rest is equivalent to laziness. While idleness can be selfish and destructive, purposeful restorative time helps us stay balanced and less prone to be triggered by negative circumstances.

Overworking ourselves can lead us to making poor decisions simply because we need a reset or time with community. If we fail to rest adequately, our body may impose a period of rest due to illness. One can only push the body so far before the alarm starts blaring and shut down procedures begin.

The Solution

Similar to the differences between energy-fillers and drainers for extroverts and introverts, what might be restful and restorative to you, might not be so for me. Resting for some is doing a puzzle, lying on the beach, baking, rafting, playing an instrument, etc. Others need to interact on some level with nature rather than indulging in an activity of solitude. Still others may be more literal and actually sleep!

The Bible is replete with examples of rest. Here are a few passages to jump start further study.

- God rested after creation. (Genesis 2:2-3)
- God set aside the Sabbath as holy and a day of rest. (Exodus 20:8-11, Exodus 23:12)
- Elijah needed food, sleep, and a special encounter with the Lord. (1 Kings 19)
- The Lord created the Sabbath for man as a refocus/reset. (Mark 2:27)
- Jesus instructed His followers to come away and rest. (Mark 6:31-32)

God created us, and He designed us with a need for rest. During these "down" times of lessened intellectual, emotional, or physical activity, we can better process information. Getting the recommended amount of sleep and taking time to get away are good for us.

If you are tired, today is a good time to take stock. How are you doing in the area of setting aside time to rest? How do you honor the Sabbath? How do you prefer to rest? How do you arrange your day/week/month/year for adequate rest to operate from an overflow rather than fumes?

Originally posted on www.bluefirelegacy.org by Dallas Henslee on 07/05/19

Learning How to Rest in the Sabbath

"The Sabbath was made for man, not man for the Sabbath." (Mark 2:27 ESV)

In early February, a few years ago, the Lord impressed upon me and my accountability partner that we were to learn about, and start practicing, a weekly Sabbath. At the time, I was running a CPA firm and he was an attorney with his own law firm. The timing of this urging is significant. Being a CPA in February meant that we had started tax season, and our busiest month of the year was right around the corner.

I had my usual monologue with the Lord, *"This wasn't a good time. How about we look at this at the end of April or in May? You just don't seem to understand . . ."* my general method of trying to convince the omniscient Creator of the universe that I knew better than Him. Nope, it didn't work.

My normal tax season schedule was to work thirteen-day weeks (taking a day off every other Sunday) through February and into March. Then as the crunch built, I'd transition to a 20-day week before the final push to April 15th. I had done this for years. It was hard but manageable, and it was what I knew. The thought of taking every Sunday off didn't seem achievable.

A Weekly Sabbath

With the help of my friend, we both committed to begin taking a day off every week. Sometimes, faith is simply being obedient to do what the Lord asks; even when our logical brain says that it may not work out. On the front end, I had my doubts and questions.

What I didn't know was that I would clock more hours that tax season than any of the prior seasons. The final seven weeks of tax season, I worked in excess of 80 hours each week. One week, I somehow put in 94 hours in six days. However, I was still able to honor the commitment to take a weekly Sabbath.

I would work Monday through Saturday. We generally stepped back from extra responsibilities such as teaching Sunday School or serving on the praise team during tax season, so on Sunday, I would get up and attend church service. After church, we would go home, and I may, or may not, eat lunch before going to nap for the afternoon. In the evening, I would get up for dinner then head to bed for the night before starting back to work early Monday morning. I'm convinced that if I didn't have one day to physically rest, I would have crashed before the finish line of the season.

The Sabbath Was Made for Us

"The Sabbath was made for man, not man for the Sabbath", (Mark 2:27, ESV). God took time to rest from work (Gen 2:2-3). Jesus also took time, regularly, to pull away from the crowds and work of ministry to rest and spend time with the Father (examples are in Matthew 14:23, Luke 5:16) in addition to being a Jew who would have practiced the weekly Sabbath.

What makes us think that we are able to go 24/7/365 without stopping regularly for rest? Generally, pride is what drives us to attempt this pace. Some of us have an inflated sense of being overly important. We may be concerned that others won't do it right, or at least, not as well as we would do it. It is also possible that we may be getting our identity from what we do, or from others, instead of who God says that we are.

We are instructed to complete all of our work in six days and rest on the seventh (Exodus 20:8-11). We like to post the ten commandments and say that they are all important, however, we often treat this fourth commandment as an optional consideration instead of necessary. If you have so much work to complete that you can't get it all done, then you are overcommitted and need to determine what you should no longer be doing. Just because there are a lot of good things doesn't mean we are supposed to be doing all of them.

A Sabbath Rest

"There remains a Sabbath rest for the people of God, for whoever has entered God's rest has also rested from his works as God did from His. Let us therefore strive to enter that rest, so that no one may fall by the same sort of disobedience", (Hebrews 4:9-11 ESV).

It is important to recognize that our rest is not in the Sabbath, rather, it is in God, Himself. If we are like the Israelites who left Egypt and proceeded to complain and test God with a spirit of disobedience, the Lord's words, "They shall not enter my rest" will also apply to us. In contrast, when we are living in obedience to His Word, we are able to enter into "God's rest".

A Sabbath rest does not have to be the same timeframe as the Jewish law dictates: from sundown Friday to sundown Saturday. While we most often have Saturday as our Sabbath, it can vary based on the work schedule. For many Christians, the Lord's Day (Sunday) is a day of rest. When engaged in ministry, Sunday is almost never a Sabbath. For planning and ease of predictability, it works best to have a regularly scheduled Sabbath day. Although, there may be a few weeks here and there that you need to have a "floating" Sabbath.

Honoring the Sabbath

What activities are allowed on the Sabbath? Rest, eating, reading, worship (not leading others), watching something enjoyable, playing games, hanging out with family, enjoying nature (not strenuous exercise related), enjoying artistic or creative pursuits that are relaxing and restorative.

What activities are not allowed on the Sabbath? Work, chores, strenuous exercise, things that are stressful or non-restful.

It is not uncommon for me to stay in my PJs all day on our Sabbath. There are some weeks that I may just sit on the couch for an extended period of time staring at a fire or nothing at all. The important thing is that I'm able to enter into the Lord's physical, emotional, mental, and spiritual rest.

Getting Started

I've heard many people say that it's impossible for them to take a day every week to rest. The reasons are as varied as the individuals. If you look, you will be able to make a list of excuses for why you cannot practice a weekly Sabbath. If you are willing to be obedient, you will be able to overcome every one of the reasons on your list.

You may need to start by setting aside four hours instead of an entire day. Start somewhere and work up to the full Sabbath. I have known several who, once making the commitment, have been able to enjoy a weekly Sabbath and, like us, can't imagine going back to the old way without it.

Originally posted on www.bluefirelegacy.org by Mark Henslee on 05/01/20

Just the Waterboy

To each is given the manifestation of the Spirit for the common good. (1 Corinthians 12:7, ESV)

There are a lot of people involved in a football game. A football team has star players, secondary players, benchwarmers, coaches, and support personnel. There are referees, scorekeepers and announcers. And yet, almost all of the attention is given to the few star players.

There seems, unfortunately, to be a similar pattern in the Church. The few superstars with name recognition sell the most books, have the largest following, and get the most praise. But the reality is, everyone in the Body of Christ has a very important role to play, and the Church cannot be who God made her to be without every one of us doing our part.

Praise of Men

I had a conversation with a worship leader where he was talking about learning how to be okay without the praise of men, including his pastor. We both acknowledged that the Lord is the ultimate approval source, and all that we do is for Him, and Him alone. However, there is the human struggle to feel unappreciated, or like we are not enough, when we don't also get some recognition from people.

This is a struggle that I know all too well. I've always been a bit odd, not normal like other people. When I was a teenager, I didn't fit in with the other youth at church or school. Over the years, I've had few friends, people that really know me. As a pastor, I was not applauded or celebrated by others, but generally, I was looked down upon or criticized for not doing things the way it's normally done. The praise of men has been rare in my life.

Yet, there are times that the Lord uses people to encourage us and give us recognition that is needed to keep going forward with His work. A rightly timed pat on the back, or "well done", can buoy us when we think what we do doesn't matter. We're still human and need some encouragement from each other. It's like the people on the sidelines cheering us on, as we take the hits from the opposing players.

Just the Waterboy

As the conversation with the worship pastor continued, I told him, "I'm just the waterboy." As ministers at Blue Fire Legacy, we're not star players, and most of the world wouldn't blink if we disappeared or even stopped our work. However, the players on the field need the waterboy. You don't see it on TV, but those kids run out onto the field between plays to get the players a drink of refreshing water. Without the constant hustle of the waterboy, the players would grow dehydrated and weary, leaving them to underperform.

We (Dallas and I / Blue Fire Legacy) are called to minister specifically to the Body of Christ. We aren't the power evangelists of the world, or the missionaries living among unreached people groups. We work with a people group that most think don't need ministry (ministers and their families). It's not a flashy ministry that garners much attention. Mostly, we work behind the scenes "off camera".

Our purpose is to "Ignite the Body of Christ to live in fullness of purity and power." There is a lot to that statement, but in short, we help ministers be emotionally and spiritually healthy, while also calling up the Church to live in accordance with Biblical standards. We bring refreshment to the players on the front lines, much like the waterboy. We also provide teaching and encouragement to the Body. My primary spiritual gift is teaching. So, I guess I'm a blend of the waterboy and the coach.

All Positions Matter

I got to tell the leader I was speaking with that day that he was a "Worship Warrior." There is a battle to be had to set the atmosphere in a service that provides the space for the preacher to speak the Word of God, and for the people to hear and receive the Word. Too often, we just think of it as a time of music, but it really is a vital part of the service. Every musician and singer on the platform needs to be doing their part to bring the people into communion with the Lord.

Paul wrote much about the many parts of the Body of Christ and how we all are important. We don't get to say that someone else is more or less important. Without everyone, the body is incomplete and suffers. See 1 Corinthians 12.

Unfortunately, many of us look at the star players and want their gifting and calling. But, if we all had the same role, there would be a whole lot missing in the church.

What Part are You?

It's not ours to determine what part of the body we are and how we contribute to the whole. That is the Lord's to do. But it is important for us to find out what our gifting and calling is from the Lord. We can't fulfill our role, if we don't know what it is.

There are a lot of spiritual gift tests available. A word of caution, these can be valuable tools, but it does not replace what God says about you. Too often, we try to live to an expectation of our own or others; instead, we need to be living for the Lord's approval.

He created each of us uniquely and specifically, as He designed. We need to walk in His design and ways, not how others think we should function. Whatever part you play, do it all to the best of your ability and for the glory of God.

Originally posted on www.bluefirelegacy.org by Mark Henslee on 07/29/22

A Desert Under the Rainforest

"May the God of hope fill you with all joy and peace in believing…." (Romans 15:13, ESV)

Praying for Rain

This year has been one of the worst drought years the area where we live has seen. Snowpacks that we depend on for runoff were measured at a very small percentage of what is required. Spring came and went, then came the wildfires, and then we noticed loads of hay being trucked in rather than out. We were told no one could remember the last time that was necessary.

I talked with one of my friends and had asked her to join us in praying for rain, especially since we were starting to see plumes of smoke from one of the fires that was 40-50 miles away. We talked about other things too, like how things were going in the ministry.

Later, she sent a text saying she had been reminded of Elijah as he prayed for rain and sent his servant seven times to check for signs of rain (1 Kings 18:41-46). On the seventh trip out to look for indications of rain, the servant returned and reported a wisp of a cloud. She wasn't positive of the exact significance, but felt she was to share.

I wasn't sure of the complete significance either, but I sensed it was less about a physical rain and more about a symbolic rain.

Dry and Parched

Shortly after that, we were listening to a sermon, and the pastor was talking about hearts that are dry and parched much like the land. He was encouraging us to ask God to water our hearts, especially those that felt dry and brittle.

Mark and I had both been struggling because it felt like the ministry had plateaued, and we weren't sure how to move forward. That, coupled with some difficult life circumstances, was weighing us down. In our experience, these seasons are easier to weather when we are not both struggling at the same time. We continued to meet with people that were looking for discipleship, encouragement and healing, and as we talked with them, it was as if God was reminding us that He is sufficient even when nothing makes sense.

Mark was out one evening on such an appointment, and I started hearing a noise I couldn't identify. What *is* that? I got up and started walking all around the house looking for the source of the sound. Then it dawned on me, and I looked up. Through the skylight, I could see water collecting on the surface.

Rain!

"It's raining!" Once I realized what the sound was, I offered up thanks to God for sending the much-needed moisture. We continued to have almost daily showers for about a week.

The irony of having prayed for rain and then not realizing what the sound was struck me and reminded me of the sermon I mentioned earlier. **What if our hearts are so dry we forget what rain, holy spiritually-renewing rain, even feels like?** Proverbs 13:12 says hope deferred can make one despondent.

"Hope deferred makes the heart sick, but a desire fulfilled is a tree of life." (ESV)

When we have lived in a place of a delayed promise, it is easy to feel as if the delay has become the death of a dream. However, if God placed the dream, He will see it through in His timing.

Wisp of a Cloud

I read somewhere that it takes 10 minutes for rain to reach the floor of the rainforest due to the dense foliage canopy. The rain has already started falling, but if you're on the ground, you won't feel it immediately because it first has to penetrate the covering layers.

We need to stay in a position of preparing and expectantly waiting. Trust me, I understand that this is not easy. I also know that God is making ready something in the delay whether it is character refining, provision, or that He be glorified even more due to the delay.

Have you missed something God was giving you because you were busy looking for a sky with an abundance of clouds instead of believing the promise of what was to come? Simply because the indicator seemed so small or the promise had been given so long ago, has your heart become dry and brittle?

When the Father sends the blessing, are you in a position to receive? Look up. Your answer may already be there in plain sight. You simply need to see it and hear it through the Truth of God's promise and faithfulness even if all you see is a wisp of a cloud.

"May the God of hope fill you with all joy and peace in believing, so that by the power of the Holy Spirit you may abound in hope." (Romans 15:13, ESV)

Originally posted on www.bluefirelegacy.org by Dallas Henslee on 11/02/18

9
Hope, Faith, and Love

Journeying From Dream to Fulfillment

The Implications of Joseph's 23 Years Before the Fulfillment of God's Promise

"I press on toward the goal for the prize of the upward call of God in Christ Jesus." (Philippians 3:14, ESV)

When we receive visions or words from the Lord about what He plans to do in and through our lives, we typically want to jump right in and go. From experience, though, I find that most often He reveals His plans, and then, He takes us through a time of preparation. This time is often quite long and sometimes includes what we may think to be a fulfillment of the word, but often isn't, the completed fulfillment.

Big Dreams

Joseph was given two dreams in his youth when he was 17 years old (Genesis 37). These dreams seemed extremely haughty, and Joseph appears very conceited when sharing them.

This is not uncommon for us today. When we are given a dream of huge things from God, we need to be careful in how we share that vision. Don't deviate from the truth of what God is revealing, but be humble in the presentation.

What are the dreams that God has given you? Where are you in the process of seeing those dreams come to fulfillment? What are you doing to be ready when the time comes?

The Great Delay

The dreams that Joseph had of his family bowing down to him didn't come to fruition until over 20 years later. We are told in Genesis 41:46 that Joseph was 30 years old when he began to serve in Pharaoh's court. Then it was another 7 years of prosperity in the land and several years of famine before his family came to Egypt for grain. So, there was 13 years from the time of the dream to the rise in power and another 10 or so years before the fulfillment of Joseph's dreams.

You may be in those years since the dream was given waiting for the fulfillment. I want to encourage you to not give up. The Lord is faithful to bring to fruition what He has called you into (1 Thessalonians 5:24). If you have lost faith in the promise, I encourage you to reconsider. Our faith is founded upon an understanding of God's promises as outlined in Scripture. Thus, He will remain faithful even when we fail (2 Timothy 2:13).

Going Down Before Going Up

So, what did Joseph do in all those years? He spent a bunch of them in low places. Literally low places, in a pit and in prison. These were the years that God used to prepare Joseph for the power that was to come to him.

There were times that I'm sure Joseph thought the end of his misery was at hand. He was promoted to the highest position in Potiphar's house. Surely this was it, he was now a man with a purpose and power. We don't know all the good, big ego things, that Joseph did in that time, but we do know that he was falsely accused of attempting to rape Potiphar's wife and thrown in prison (Genesis 39:11-20).

It is very common to have someone accuse us of doing what they are guilty of when we don't go along with their plans. Potiphar's wife tried to seduce Joseph multiple times. Joseph was faithful to his employer and did not concede to the affair. So, as a woman scorned, she accused him of what she was doing. False accusation which led to the dismissal from his position of purpose and power. It could have led to his execution, but God was in control even if at the time Joseph probably didn't feel such.

Our Response to the Circumstances

How do we respond when circumstances don't line up with our expectations? I've seen many Christians throw a huge, "God you don't care about me; I am better than this; I don't desire this; I'm not supposed to be here; how could You let this happen to me; You don't love me" pity party, or temper tantrum. I've had my share of those "parties". We don't know if Joseph had one or not, but we do know that he didn't stay there and neither should we.

Discipline is never pleasant, but it is vital for our growth. The Lord loves us so much that He doesn't leave us where we are at. He wants to grow us into mature children who are able to share in His holiness. He desires that we produce a harvest of righteousness. (See Hebrews 12:4-11).

Back in prison, Joseph quickly rose to the position of a trusted manager. He didn't have freedom, he didn't have power over his own life, he didn't have much at all, but he did have a calling from God to manage others. So that is what he did. He became a faithful manager, in a prison, at a low point in his life. God used him where he was to foster growth in preparation for the fulfillment of the divine dream from years prior.

Likewise, we are to do what we are gifted and called to do, even if it is at a place or level that isn't where we believe we should be serving. Learn to be faithful in the little things and the low places.

Being Moldable

God was working all the way through Joseph's story. Before Joseph could be the manager of the entire country of Egypt, he needed to learn how to manage a household and then a prison. Skills that I'm sure he learned in those positions were invaluable and essential for the later position.

God had called Joseph to an incredibly large position, but first, He needed to prepare him. When we are first introduced to Joseph in Genesis 37, he is a young, know-it-all, pain-in-the-neck, arrogant, conceited, spoiled brat. God had a lot of work to do before Joseph would be ready to fulfill that calling. In those 13 years of pits, prisons and false starts, God was molding Joseph into a humble, educated, skilled manager with good character.

For me, the biggest lesson that God's been working on in my life is humility. When I was young, I tended to be a know-it-all, arrogant brat. I was successful in business and looked up to in that world. Then the Lord asked me to give up that identity for something else. It hasn't been an easy process. Humility never is obtained easily, but I know that in the end it is good.

False Starts

At some point in his time of prison "ministry", I'm sure Joseph thought he had his way out. He gave a great dream interpretation to the cupbearer of Pharaoh. Surely this was his ticket. The cupbearer would tell Pharaoh how great he was and that he was innocent and should be let out. But that didn't happen. "Two full years later" (Genesis 41:1) the cupbearer remembered Joseph. Two years of amnesia? How on earth could someone not remember the man who told him he was going to get out of prison and go back to his trusted position serving Pharaoh? We aren't told, but I'm thinking that Joseph had a few negative thoughts towards that cupbearer in those two years. Probably even a few negative thoughts towards God. Possibly even feelings of abandonment.

A false summit is that place when you are going uphill that you think is the top of the climb. Only when you get there do you find that there is more to go. When we are growing toward our dream, we are likely to find a false summit or two, or five or twelve, along the way. Places where we are *sure* that we've finally made it through the tough stuff and can celebrate some victories. Where the process will become easier and "all will be smooth sailing from here."

Think about the last false summit you encountered. How did you respond? How do you wish you had responded?

When you reach a false summit, it's okay to stop and take a breather for a few minutes. Just don't stop too long. Don't get discouraged with the climb, instead celebrate the victory of what has been accomplished. Look back and recount the progress made while praising and thanking the Lord for His faithfulness along the way.

Stepping Up Into the Calling

In time, and probably not when we planned or expected, the doors will open, and we will be walking in the calling that was given all those years earlier. When that occurs, we need to make the transition well.

We're told that Joseph had to shave and get cleaned up when he was called before Pharaoh. When we are called up, we need to be willing to clean up nicely. That may mean shaving and changing clothes as Joseph did, or it may mean changing things that we do. The important thing is that we are willing to "dress" the part that God is calling us into. We need to be willing to wear the mantle that God has designed for us.

God Cares About the Journey

The rest of Joseph's story is the fulfillment of the dream that he had as a youth. One can read the entire story (Genesis 37 - 47) in less than an hour, but it took Joseph *decades* to live it. We need to remember this when we are in the midst of our life story. So often, we want to speed up to the fulfillment, but God is more interested in the process. We want the purpose and power; He wants our devotion. He is more interested in our character than our position; our heart than our circumstances; and in our relationship with Him than anything else. Our journey with God is of utmost importance.

Wherever you are on your journey from the dream to fulfillment, know that God is there walking with you. Don't give up. Even on those hard days; know that He is good. Don't let circumstances dictate your outlook. As Paul encourages in Philippians 3:12-14, Press on toward the calling of the Lord all the way to the realization of the dream come true! And enjoy the journey with Him.

Originally posted on www.bluefirelegacy.org by Mark Henslee on 07/28/18

How to Find an Auto Mechanic by Listening

"And your ears shall hear a word behind you, saying, "This is the way, walk in it," when you turn to the right or when you turn to the left." (Isaiah 30:21, ESV)

In the summer of 2016, one of our daughters had a check engine light come on in her car. She took it to a national brand repair shop who quoted an exorbitant price for repair. I knew that I would be in Houston the following week, so I told her to tell them thanks but that she would get a second opinion. I prayed for the next week that the Lord would guide me to a trustworthy mechanic that not only could do this work but also be a source for any future needs.

The Search Begins

I asked a few people in the area if they knew a good, trustworthy mechanic, but no one did. Seems odd that all these people don't have a mechanic that they trust. I guess I'm odd in that I tend to drive older, high mileage cars and build a relationship with my mechanic.

Before getting to Houston, I told Dallas that I thought I knew which direction I was supposed to go from Gabrielle's apartment, but that was all I had gotten from the Lord. The day came, and I started off down Rice Street. I was driving in the left lane with a city bus in the right lane just ahead of me. A little way down, I got the impression that I was supposed to get in the right lane.

In my desire to not be behind the bus, I didn't move over right away. At the next light, I had to stop. The bus also had to stop and did so short of the light, about a car's length. There, on the corner, was an old, faded sign that read, "Bellaire Auto Repair" with an arrow pointing down the street to the right. Since I hadn't immediately listened when I was impressed to get into the right lane, I had to go down to the next street and then circle back. Note that God had caused the bus driver to stop short of the light so that I could see the sign.

Success!

Once I circled back to the corner with the sign, I began looking for a Bellaire Auto, but there were no auto shops right there. So, I figured the sign and arrow were directional, and I drove down the street. Not too far down, I saw an auto repair shop and got the impression that I had arrived. On the wall was a sign that read, "Tommy King's Auto Repair: Serving Bellaire since 1973" along with an ASE sign and a listing of services, all of which fit what I was hoping to find.

I got out of the car and walked up to the mechanic that was working under the hood of an SUV. He greeted me, and we began the conversation about what was needed. Turns out, he was the head mechanic at the shop. He listened, advised and genuinely wanted to help. During the conversation, we went into the office so that I could write down my information for the office manager to call me with a quote. It was a surprise to look in the back shop area and see quite a few classic cars along with later model cars. It turns out that Tommy King's clientele is primarily doctors and lawyers with toys. We don't really fit as their normal clients, but the low pressure, family feel of the place fits us.

When we went back a little later to leave the car, we met the office manager and also the owner's daughter. We spent a little time visiting, mostly surface stuff. I told her that whether she knew it or not they were an answer to prayer. She looked a little unsure about how to take that comment but seemed okay. I guess that many people would hear a story like this and think that I'm just a bit off.

Lessons on Hearing God

On the way back to the apartment, I got to share with my daughter how I found the shop. One of the big points that I've had to learn in hearing God is that we don't get a big choir of angels or a nice clear audible voice. Scripture tells us that the Lord speaks in a still small voice. I would say that it is much less of a voice and more of a prompting or knowing inside; others might say it's an impression. I've tried to figure out how to explain it, but it really is something other than humanly normal. How did I know to go south? Well, I just did. Why did I know that I needed to get in the right lane? Not sure, but I knew it. The sign on the corner was a bit more obvious.

Even when we miss it, like when I didn't get behind the bus, God is kind and gracious to give us another chance. However, if we are purposeful in ignoring His promptings, then He will honor our request and leave us to our choices. Obedience is a choice that we get to make through each step of life.

Something else to know is that sometimes the Lord uses the physical to speak to us, like with the sign. It is important that we not limit Him to our methods and our ways. I find in Scripture that Jesus performed healings in multiple ways and rarely (if ever) did He do something in the same manner. God is interested in a personal relationship, and therefore, He personalizes how he relates to each of us.

Putting it Into Practice

For bigger life decisions, it is wise to seek Godly counsel for confirmation in addition to praying about it. Something like finding a mechanic is different than selling everything and going into a specific ministry. The Lord will speak; we need to be sure it is Him and not ourselves.

No matter what is in front of you, if you sincerely seek the Lord's direction, He will answer. You may have to quiet your life to hear. Too often, we let the busyness and chaos of life drown out His voice. Keep in mind, when He does speak, you will likely have to adjust your path to get where He is leading you.

Is the Lord speaking to you? Are you in a place to hear Him when he does speak? Are you choosing to walk in obedience?

Originally posted on www.bluefirelegacy.org by Mark Henslee on 11/16/18

When You are Lost, Look for the Avalanche

"But he knows the way that I take; when he has tried me, I shall come out as gold. My foot has held fast to his steps; I have kept his way and have not turned aside.

(Job 23:10-11)

Back on July 1st, my dog, Ginger, and I were continuing our quest to get to a high mountain lake. We had made several attempts in June, but the snow levels prevented us from making it all the way. Today was going to be the day. After all, it was now July so surely the snow would have melted enough.

We set out across Rainbow Trail and then up Goodwin Lake Trail. Aside from the many trees that had fallen across the trail, we were making good time. Then, less than a mile from the lakes, the snow became deeper and completely covered the trail. But I was determined and used some basic navigation skills to keep going.

We ended up above the lake which provided a beautiful view that we wouldn't have otherwise gotten. After lunch beside the clear waters, it was time to head back home. The problem was that the trail was completely covered and going back the way we came wasn't the ideal solution. Somehow, I had to figure out how to find the trail again.

An Avalanche Saves the Day

A couple miles below the lake, there was an avalanche that had gone across the trail. On the way up, I had taken a picture of the debris field as it was an amazing sight to see. Since the avalanche had made a roughly 150- to 200-foot-wide path of destruction down the side of the mountain, I figured that if I found it, I could find the trail.

I knew to follow the creek running out of the lake, so I started down. Staying on the upper side of the creek, I headed to find my avalanche.

After some adjustments for fallen trees and steep drops, we came out into the avalanche's debris field. Now where was the trail? Fortunately, I was able to look at the picture and figure out where I was standing in relation to the downed trees. It took me a while as the view from below (where I took the picture) was different from where I was above, but sure enough, we found the trail.

Lost in Life

As we journey through life, we are going to have events and circumstances that cause us to lose our way. I'm guessing that I'm not the only one who gets lost in the emotions, relationships, and circumstances of life.

It may be good things in life: Graduating high school and heading out on your own, getting married, having kids, becoming an empty nester, parenting adult children, etc. These are all good things, but when you encounter them, the trail ahead may be unclear.

It could be difficulties that try to knock us out: The loss of a loved one, being fired from a job, a major illness, the betrayal of a friend. When difficult situations cover the trail, how do we find our way again?

Look for the Avalanche

The good Sunday School answer is to pray and trust the Lord. While prayer and trust are essential, we need to *do* something. Sitting in our misery doesn't move us forward. Besides, who wants to be lost on the mountainside?

Maybe you can phone a friend. The value of a friend that can listen and help you navigate the situations of life is priceless. Unfortunately, your friend may not be on the mountain with you and able to help find the trail.

Think about Job's friends. They meant well, but they truly could not relate to the depth of Job's loss. Some of what they had to say was actually harmful instead of helpful.

Sometimes, when you are on the mountain alone, you need to go back to a significant place in the past. I call them milestones. A time when God spoke so clearly; an anchor of faith.

Healing the Destruction

Sometimes, to move forward, we have to go to places of deep hurt that haven't been healed. Much like the avalanche caused a field of destruction and debris, we all have experienced hurts. It may be a time when a friend stabbed you in the back, piercing your heart, or you were abused, or you had a moral failure. Some hurts are bigger than others, but they all matter.

In our work with ministers and their families, we spend a lot of time looking for the roots of the symptoms and finding healing for those past hurts. The path forward almost always requires healing from a past event.

Forgiveness is one of the biggest keys to healing. The process of forgiveness is not easy, but it is well worth the work. Unforgiveness is effectively a prison that we are held in, and we have the key to get out. To learn more about forgiveness, you can read our book, *Breaking the Burdensome Yoke: A Discipleship Course in Forgiving and Grieving*.

In addition to forgiveness, we may need to deal with other aspects of the hurt. There may be a need to clean up the emotional attachments of the memories, or there may be flesh bonds and soul ties that need to be broken. Some of us carry great weights of shame from our past that we need to give to God. Others have guilt that keeps them firmly anchored in the past and unable to move forward in life. Whatever you are burdened with, the Lord is more than able to provide you freedom and hope.

Walk It Out

What are the avalanches in your life? Are they places that provide security and bolster your faith? Do you have places that need healing?

Our past experiences of trials and victory can be like the picture I took, providing perspective and ability to regroup. Because God is consistent and faithful in character, we can depend on Him for our healing. He really enjoys walking with us through the journey of life.

Originally posted on www.bluefirelegacy.org by Mark Henslee on 11/22/19

When Free Parking Isn't So Fun

"And Samuel said, 'Has the LORD as great delight in burnt offerings and sacrifices, as in obeying the voice of the LORD? Behold, to obey is better than sacrifice, and to listen than the fat of rams.'" (1 Samuel 15:22, ESV)

Shortly after we moved to a suburb of Colorado Springs to assist with a church startup project, I met a worship leader that was lamenting that he felt like he had been put on a shelf by God. Ironically, he was teaching me how to be a better worship leader from behind the keyboard at that time.

In retrospect, I think God was protecting him from committing to a leadership role in the church plant and uprooting his life to move to another state just in time for the project to disband completely. However, I do empathize with his feelings of being shelved and not actively used in ministry.

Parked

As I write this memory to share with you, we are literally parked. We had anticipated being able to just keep going without any real interruption to the ministry or our timetable. Boy, were we wrong!

First, in the midst of moving and transitioning from the house to the 5th wheel, we were both slammed with COVID. Mark says losing two weeks of our lives certainly didn't help in the timeline department. I'd have to agree.

Second, because of the timing of illness, we were unable to access our annual networking conference which tends to refuel us emotionally to do the work we do with others. Due to the complete cancellation of the event last year, it has been over two years since we have been able to pull away and re-energize through this means.

Third, we are currently stalled in regards to moving forward. It was our intention, and hope, to be headed to Texas for the winter several days ago. This is obviously not the case, since I stated earlier that we are currently parked. We are in our ministry 5th wheel, in a church parking lot, awaiting God's provision of a truck, large enough to transport the trailer.

Waiting and Transition

We have not wasted the time, but we are anxious to get moving again. In all candor, some of this is an emotional response. For the second time in six years, we've placed the majority of our pared down belongings into storage.

The first time, we were homeless for 54 weeks. This time, there is stability in having our own living space, however, the uncertainty of the future remains the same. The first time, we awoke in a small family/community property camper to temperatures inside registering in the 30s Fahrenheit. This time around, we're mostly able to maintain a comfortable temperature overnight. (The exception being last night when the propane ran out and it was 48 degrees inside).

We have continued to schedule client meetings and have even held an in-person appointment locally in the new accommodations, since moving out of our house. The space is tight but doable. Part of the "put on the shelf" feeling for us, is that we'd like to be doing more teaching and growing that arm of the ministry while helping to balance the emotional toll of the coaching and inner healing work that we offer (most simply call these counseling appointments for ease of relatability).

We have also been plugging away at the renovations in the 5th wheel that we had hoped would be complete prior to moving in. We're definitely gaining ground on the long to do list. Mark got the hot water heater working. We only had to go one day without it. I'm thankful for the opportunity to take hot showers even if there is an on/off procedure required to have sufficient hot water to last the entire shower.

Heartache Even in Obedience

Not only are our hands, fingers, and other parts of our body sore from all the renovation work, but our hearts are experiencing the ache of having to surrender desires. The desire to be with family for Thanksgiving. The desire to have a ministry truck and be independently able to transport the 5th wheel as the need arises. The desire to be increasing the number of speaking/teaching engagements and decreasing the number of counseling commitments.

"And Samuel said, 'Has the LORD as great delight in burnt offerings and sacrifices, as in obeying the voice of the LORD? Behold, to obey is better than sacrifice, and to listen than the fat of rams.'" (1 Samuel 15:22, ESV)

As much as God desires obedience rather than sacrifice, it is all too easy for the enemy to start messing in my thoughts when I'm walking in obedience but struggling with the sacrifice required.

"Haven't you done everything He asked; then why are you still here?"

"What did you miss or leave undone?"

"Does He really love you enough to provide what you've asked for?"

"What you do doesn't matter; you're easily overlooked."

When the enemy does that; I have to be alert enough to take every thought captive and evaluate it against the truth of Scripture.

Back to the Beginning

See, the thing is, in being obedient, there is often an element of surrender. Surrender feels very much like personal sacrifice. If we are willingly sacrificial to the point of obedience, there is an expectation that He'll bless such actions, shower us with favor, and even "unstick" us. Conditional obedience comes from skewed heart intent. An attitude of, "I'll do this because if I do, He'll do that (which is usually something to our benefit)." God chooses to bless His children, but He does so in a way that brings Him glory rather than in a way that enables an entitlement spirit.

Getting back to our circumstances and surrendering from earlier.... While we had come to terms with the likelihood of not being with family for Thanksgiving, and even remaining stuck until the first part of December, God chose to write the story another way. He honored the willingness without requiring it of us.

Originally posted on www.bluefirelegacy.org by Dallas Henslee on 12/01/21

Six Keys for Implementing Change in Your Life

"Faith is the assurance of things hoped for, the conviction of things not seen." (Hebrews 11:1, ESV)

When we enter a period of change in life, there are some things that we need to be aware of and prepared to address. We see six keys for implementing change when we look at the Israelites' story as they were told to leave Egypt and take possession of the Promised Land (Exodus 1 - 17, Numbers 11 - 14 and 20 - 22, and Joshua 1 - 11).

1) Listen without an agenda
2) Exercise faith in the face of doubt
3) Take action to implement
4) Be obedient to the Lord's instructions
5) Persevere through the difficulties
6) Take possession of the promises

Let's take a deeper look into each of these keys for attaining positive change in life.

Listen Without an Agenda

God gave Moses and Joshua instructions for each step of the process. Some of the instructions were very specific while others were more generalized. However, He didn't give them every step upfront. Throughout, they were required to be in constant communication with the Lord. So, too, it is for us.

We must be in constant prayer. Not just petitioning prayer, but rather, *listening* prayer. We need to be in the Word. We need to be in communion with other believers. The Holy Spirit speaks, but do we listen? Are we positioned to listen?

It is important to be sure we filter what others say through the Word and the Holy Spirit. Many well-intentioned people giving rational thoughts have led people out of the Lord's will. Throughout the process of going from Egypt to the Promised Land, God told the Israelites to do some very non-rational things. Sometimes, He will do the same with us today. If we only listen to the rational, we are likely to miss the miracles.

Jesus tells us that His sheep know His voice (John 10:4). We must know the Lord's voice so that we know what to listen to and follow. This requires more of that listening prayer.

As we receive each instruction, we need to be willing to follow it. We must also continue to listen for further instructions. Sometimes, we get the entire process up front, but in my experience, God generally gives one or two steps at a time. Maybe it's because I might run ahead of Him or get them out of order. Listening is an ongoing process.

Exercise Faith in the Face of Doubt

The Lord gave the promise of deliverance into the Promised Land, but the leaders had to lead in faith. And, they had to lead the people forward even when the circumstances didn't look promising. Are we willing to walk forward even when everything around us appears difficult?

Hebrews 11:1, ESV tells us, "Faith is the assurance of things hoped for, the conviction of things not seen." Often, when the Lord speaks to us, we don't see how it is possible for that word to come to fruition. We must not rely on our own reason, understanding, or what we see. We must rely on the Word of the Lord.

Some think that if we have faith that means that we never doubt. I hope that is not true, because as I've walked in great processes of faith, I have still had doubts along the way. I believe that faith is the ability to continue to press on in the face of doubt. Doubt is rooted in the circumstances, while faith is grounded in God's character and promises.

Faith is not walking by what we see. Faith is walking in *Who* we believe. Our eyes can be very deceiving when it comes to things of God's Kingdom. The Father, however, is always dependable regardless of the circumstances.

Take Action to Implement

It is not enough to receive the instructions and have faith, we must take action. Moses could have built an altar and worshiped the burning bush because that was where Yahweh revealed Himself. If that were the case, no change would have happened except for Moses being an idolater.

Too often, we hear the Lord, believe Him, and then stop there. We like to talk about what the Lord said to us. This great revelation that He gave.

Instead of just talking, we must walk. Moses had to go stand before Pharaoh, the people had to ask their neighbors for jewelry and clothing, the Levites had to walk into the swollen Jordan River, the people had to walk around the city of Jericho for seven days, and on and on. There were actions required.

What are the actions that you need to take? Whether large or small, it is important to take those steps that we have been instructed to take. Even when (or especially when) they are difficult.

Be Obedient to the Lord's Instructions

The Lord requires obedience. Not just to the initial instructions but specific obedience to everything that He tells us to do. Too often, we receive instructions, follow them and they work out, so we think that is how we need to do it the next time.

Consider Moses striking the rocks for water (Exodus 17:1-7 and Numbers 20:2-13). The first time, the Lord had told him to strike the rock, but the second time, he was instructed to speak to the rock. We cannot rely upon yesterday's instructions but must continually be in communication with the Lord for today's task.

Did the water come out of the rock the second time when Moses struck it instead of speaking to it? Yes. However, the negative consequence for Moses because of disobedience was significant. He wasn't allowed to cross the Jordan and live in the Promised Land! Obedience is vital for us to walk in the complete provision and blessing of the Lord.

Back to the entire narrative, each of the battles to take possession of the land (Jericho, Ai, etc.) had different techniques required. Why? Because obedience is of utmost importance to God. As Samuel said to Saul in 1 Samuel 15:22, ESV, "Has the Lord as great delight in burnt offerings and sacrifices, as in obeying the voice of the Lord? Behold, to obey is better than sacrifice, and to listen than the fat of rams." (See also Hosea 6:6, Hebrews 10:5-8). The Lord desires to walk in relationship with us, over us simply following a set of do and don't rules.

The act of unhindered obedience is more pleasing to God than any work we think we need to do to please Him. Obedience best comes from a place of relationship with the Father. We want to please Him because of who He is and who we are in relationship with each other.

Persevere Through the Difficulties

We often expect that once we start down the path of obedience and faith the road will become smooth and easy. Scripture does NOT support that expectation. (Sorry to burst your bubble.) There will be obstacles, battles, times where it seems all is lost, times we think we missed the calling, doubt and, in general, hard stuff.

As soon as we make the decision to walk forward in the Lord's instructions (regardless of how much we understand), the enemy will rise up against us. Spiritual warfare is real. We need to be aware of, and prepared to battle in, the spirit realm, as well as persevere in the physical.

The enemy doesn't fight fair, nor does he give up easily. Often, we have to command him and his minions to back off, get out, or stop what they are doing more than once. For more information about spiritual warfare check out our book *Behind Enemy Lines: A Discipleship Course in Spiritual Warfare*.

Perseverance is not easy. Another name for it is long-suffering, which sounds even worse. There may be days that it seems like all is lost. Other days may feel like you have failed miserably. Through it all, we must keep our eyes, ears, and heart focused on the Lord. He is more than able, and we are more than conquerors through Him (Romans 8:37).

Take Possession of the Promises

It is not enough just to win. When the battles are won, we must take possession of the territory that the Lord has brought us into.

If we don't live in the land, then the wild animals will take over control. The Lord didn't go before the Israelites and clear the land. He gave it to them as they were able to possess and settle it (Exodus 23:29).

For the completion of the change process, we must possess the new territory. When you make changes, there will be a time of adjustment and learning to live in the new place. It is often easy to revert back to the old things whether that is a physical place or manners of operating (habits, thought patterns, etc.). We must not allow this to happen.

We have the option to refuse to step forward in faith. The Lord will allow us to wander in the wilderness until the next generation is ready to step up. That doesn't mean He wants us to, but He chose to grant us free will. We must live with the consequences of our decisions if we choose to be disobedient. God doesn't live within the boundaries of time like we do. He is infinitely patient, and He has infinite resources to carry out His will.

What happens when we aren't obedient in the Lord's instructions and don't *take action* to possess the promise? Does He sit up in Heaven and fret about it? No. We lose out, but the Lord's promises do get fulfilled, just by others. When the spies came back and the people listened to the ten over the two, they made the decision to miss the promise. The Lord still gave the Promised Land to the nation of Israel, He just waited to give it to the next generation.

Originally posted on www.bluefirelegacy.org by Mark Henslee on 07/29/18

The Mercy of "No" and "Not Yet"

> *"But he said to me, 'My grace is sufficient for you, for my power is made perfect in weakness.' Therefore I will boast all the more gladly of my weaknesses, so that the power of Christ may rest upon me."* (2 Corinthians 12:9, ESV)

When Mark and I were stepping out in faith to establish Blue Fire Legacy, we were given several heads-up impressions from the Lord so we could prepare and be ready. I often tell people about my two-year warning about packing the house to move in the context of having to learn to listen more closely to timing prompts.

It was a season of multiple ongoing changes. One of which, we thought, was that God was asking us to downsize from a 5 bedroom/3 ½ bathroom home to live in a Class A Diesel Pusher full-time. We would lie awake at night discussing the desired features after having looked at several on-line and in person. Blue on the exterior, rich dark cherry cabinets, at least 3 slides, a bath & ½ for when we held appointments, a dishwasher….

We also discussed what we were going to do with our furniture, family photos, etc. Most things I was willing to part with, but there were a few sentimental pieces of furniture that I wanted to keep. I didn't wind up keeping all those pieces; my piano was one of the ones surrendered.

When it was time, we purged our belongings by selling, giving away, throwing away, re-evaluating what was left, and then started the process all over again. By the way, I'm simply NOT a garage sale kind of gal so this was a tedious task for sure. Once we had pared down to what we felt we could keep, we arranged for storage.

Pursuing the RV

Then, we pursued the RV, but there were no funds. Even when we received RV contributions, we maxed out at $4000. There isn't much available in that price range, and the vehicles that are for sale in the low dollar range need major renovations. In light of the realization that we were not able to purchase an RV for the ministry, we really struggled with questions like,

> "Did we misunderstand God's instructions?"
>
> "Did we completely miss it?"
>
> "Did we do something wrong?"

One day, as I was pondering all of this, I came to the place of recognition that His "No" for the RV we wanted, was actually a very merciful answer that in reality is, "Not yet."

Character Testing and Refining

There was a lot of character testing and refining occurring, but it was more about our willingness than anything else. He is pleased with our willingness to live full-time in an RV but did not require the sacrifice of us. He knows us better than we know ourselves. That includes knowing our personality inclinations toward a home base, a place to come back to and rejuvenate, reconnect with community, etc. We still downsized, but He miraculously provided a small home we could purchase outright.

We believe strongly that the RV is still a coming provision and resource for the ministry. There are pieces of what we are called to do through Blue Fire Legacy that necessitate travel and extended lodging. In this case, the mercy of the answer "not yet" prevented us from paying money we didn't have for insurance, storage, and upkeep on a vehicle we were not yet positioned to utilize.

The Answer May Really be No

There are instances when God definitively says, "No." It isn't like the circumstances above where it is an instruction to wait.

God told David he couldn't build the Temple. It was a clear, "No." with a reason. (1 Chronicles 17:1-4, 22:1-19, & 28:1-21)

God told Jesus, "No" when Jesus asked if there was a way he could avoid suffering death on the cross. (Luke 22:39-43)

God told Paul, "No" when Paul asked that the thorn in his side be removed. (2 Corinthians 12:7-10)

God may tell you, "No" when you ask for a specific job, when you ask to be removed from difficult circumstances, or even when you ask for a loved one to be healed. The answer may be no because He is completing what He started in you. The answer may be no because He is providing for another through you. None of us would have the gift of salvation if Jesus had opted out. God's answer may be no because He wants you to learn Who He truly is. With Paul, He said, "My grace is sufficient…." (2 Corinthians 12:9, NIV) Paul would not have learned to depend on God's sufficiency in the absence of difficulty.

God told us no when we attempted to buy a house closer to Mark's office several years ago. At that point, we didn't realize that we would be going into full-time ministry. It would have been an additional hardship for us had the sale gone through. He said no other times like when changing phone service providers would have been unwise and when going on a mission trip would have created logistical and emotional stress at home. He sees the big picture, and there are times when "no" is the absolute best answer, even if, in the moment, it disappoints us.

Seeking an Answer

Are there areas in your life that you received a no or not yet from God and you still feel heartbroken because He didn't make you more comfortable by fulfilling your wish or signing your pre-drawn-up contract? Perhaps there is discovery of His mercy and heart for you in the answer. I encourage you to seek it out.

Originally posted on www.bluefirelegacy.org by Dallas Henslee on 02/07/20

Planning International Travel by Prayer and Faith

"And this is the confidence that we have toward him, that if we ask anything according to his will he hears us."

(1 John 5:14, ESV)

In the summer of 2018, we felt like we were to go to Bangladesh to visit a missionary couple. Mark looked at airlines and flights but didn't really spend much time on it. In December 2018, we sensed that the time was getting close, and we should talk with them about when would be good to visit and then start planning. In January 2019, it was determined that March would be the best time.

So, we did what we thought God was telling us to do. We started telling people that we were going to Bangladesh in March. We blocked March 4th to 19th on our calendar to go, not having any resources or ability to actually make the trip happen. As a general principle, we don't ask for funds, but instead, pray for the Father to provide, making the need known through our emailed newsletter. After the January newsletter went out, we received two donations towards the trip. Then, we received nothing else for all of February. What we had was certainly not enough to be able to buy plane tickets.

Praying it Through

In early February, Dallas was speaking with a supporter on the phone when they mentioned the possibility of assisting with airline tickets using their frequent flyer miles. For simplicity and anonymity, we'll call them John and Jane going forward. Jane was quite busy that week, so she said it could be a while before she could look into it. Dallas informed Mark, and we added this potential to our prayer list.

On Thursday, February 14th, we were praying over the trip, and Mark specifically prayed, "If John and Jane are supposed to help facilitate the trip, please lay it on her heart to look at it today." That night, we received a text message with some general flight options. After texting back and forth for a while, Jane was ready to put flights on hold. Then, we received a text, "Pray harder". So, we did. After a bit, we were told that all of the flights had disappeared. It was very late (after midnight her time), and she had to give up and go to bed. While a bit confused, we realized that the Lord had answered our specific prayer – she looked at flights and let us know.

For the next week, our prayer was for the Lord to put it on Jane's heart when she was supposed to get back to the flight plans. Meanwhile, we were also asking for the Lord to provide the funds needed to purchase the portion of the tickets that would not be covered by miles plus the ancillary expenses associated with traveling.

A Dream

On Thursday, February 21, Dallas woke up and shared that she had a dream the night before. The scene was her standing at our kitchen sink and the house phone ringing. The unidentified person on the other end of the phone indicated that the tickets were purchased. While Dallas was thankful in the moment, she almost forgot to mention it the next morning.

Getting There

That same evening, we received an email with information for flights that Jane had placed on hold. We had told Jane that our dates of departure and return were flexible and to look for flights from Denver, Colorado. However, she had held a flight from Dallas/Ft. Worth, Texas (DFW) on March 4th, returning from Dhaka, Bangladesh to DFW on March 19th. Those were the exact dates that we had blocked on our calendar back in January. It was of interest to us that the flights were from and to Dallas instead of Denver as we were looking at the possibility of taking Mark's 4Runner to our daughter in the Dallas area. In which case, it would work great for us to fly out of DFW.

Friday, February 22, we had a call with Jane to discuss the held flights. That evening, we were able to find a flight from Denver with the same DFW to DAC legs at the same cost. So, we released the hold from Dallas and placed a hold on the flight from Denver. This allowed us the time to determine if we needed to take the car to our daughter or not, as she had an appointment with a second mechanic the next day.

Saturday morning, February 23rd, Mark had the thought that if there was a flight from Denver, maybe there was one from Colorado Springs. Upon looking, there was, so he wrote an email to Jane requesting that she switch the hold to that flight. Before sending the email, we had a call from our daughter and determined that we did not need to drive a car down to the Dallas area after all. A few word changes, and we sent the email requesting that Jane book the flights from COS to DAC leaving March 4th, which she did that day.

What About Getting Home?

You may notice in this narrative that we only booked flights to get *to* Bangladesh. While we had a flight on hold to return to DFW, the supporters didn't have enough miles to purchase them, and we didn't have enough funds to buy the additional miles needed. Most people would not book international travel halfway around the world without the ability to book the flights to get back home. Needless to say, we're not normal people, nor has God asked us to operate in the natural, common ways of man.

There was the offer to go ahead and book the return flights that day with John and Jane covering the difference in the cost. This seemed very reasonable, and generous of them, but both of us felt like we were supposed to wait. So, we kindly declined the offer, and asked Jane to wait as we continued to pray. To which she replied that she would wait, and "God works in mysterious ways!"

Willing to Wait

I would like to emphasize that through the process of praying for the Lord to provide, we did not actively request funds. We simply stated in our monthly email newsletters that we would be going to Bangladesh in March as the Lord provided. We're learning the incredible power of prayer and dependence on the Lord. It is an awesome thing to come before the Creator of the universe with something as simple as airline tickets and for Him to answer those prayers in ways we could not have imagined.

At one point, Dallas even said to Mark, "Do you think we may have to pack and go to the airport before the tickets are available?" We've heard about missionaries who would do that before 9/11, but we're not sure how that would work in today's world. Regardless, if the Lord asks us to do that, we're willing to go there.

Also of note, is that we did not have any sense of concern that the trip was not going to happen. While our natural minds did not grasp the way in which it could occur, we knew in our hearts that we were going and that we would also be returning. The willingness to trust the Lord's directions regardless of what we see is of utmost importance in our faith journey.

Acting on Promptings

On Monday, February 25th, Mark was working on his computer and suddenly had an urgency to check for return flights from Dhaka to Colorado. Lo and behold, there was a flight returning to COS which had never been available in previous searches. He emailed the information to Jane and requested that she put the return flight on hold. Within a short time, she responded with the hold confirmation for a return flight to Colorado which was good until Saturday, March 2nd. This was a big deal because the originally held flights to DFW would necessitate at least a couple hundred more dollars in flights back to Colorado plus additional hassle and travel time.

With tickets booked for departure, it was rather urgent to finalize dog sitters for three weeks. We thought we had about two weeks covered but, because the final week was Spring break for the local schools, finding someone to cover that time was proving to be rather difficult. Through prayer, we believe that the Lord made the connections for the third sitter on Thursday, February 28th. Yes, that was just three short days before we were to leave home to start the journey. We met two of the sitters and introduced them to the dogs and the care needed on Saturday, March 2nd.

A Brief Panic

Remember that return flight that was held until March 2nd? Well, it is important to note what time zone a flight hold is good for as our flight was held until midnight in Bangladesh, which is 10 hours later than our supporters' location (and 13 hours different from CO). You guessed it. We lost the held flights because they weren't booked in time.

We have to admit that despite knowing we were going and that God had everything taken care of, we did have a few minutes of panic. Mark pulled out the computer to search for other possible flights, and there was absolutely nothing available the entire month back to COS or DEN. After a prayer, it was decided that we had zero ability to make the return trip happen. Therefore, we turned it over to the Lord and continued working on packing and getting ready to leave the next day.

As is His way, God did resolve the situation with a return flight option traveling through Hong Kong instead of Doha. Call us weird if you want, but this was rather intriguing and exciting. You see, this flight meant that we would *literally* be flying around the world on the trip. An added bonus was that the departure time from Dhaka would be easier on us and our hosts. Jane had put this flight on hold until March 7th pending our approval to book.

God Protects Us From Our Ignorance

We are still relatively new to the whole international travel routine, and therefore, are still learning some things about how it works. We knew that we needed a return itinerary before we could get our entrance visa into Bangladesh (about 7 am on March 6th). What we have since learned is that before we could even board the flight in Colorado on Monday morning March 4th, we needed to have that return flight booked.

Fortunately, God is a good Father who takes care of His children in our ignorance. Since we had booked the tickets to go, John had flown more (he does that, *a lot*). Sunday morning, Jane texted that we were about 5,000 miles short but that he was flying again that afternoon. We presumed from her message that surely by the 7th there would be enough to book the tickets without having to buy any miles. We already had enough funds to cover the taxes and fees, so we were good.

By God's grace, John's miles from the Sunday flight were posted to the account early Monday morning, which apparently does not usually happen so quickly. Jane booked the flights about *two hours* before we were to arrive at the airport to depart. We were able to print the itinerary at our daughter's house, where we had spent the night, prior to leaving which became rather handy when we were checking in for the flight. Even though we didn't know all the rules, God made it possible for us to comply and pass through with ease.

Continued Provisions

Friday and Saturday, we had a couple of glitches. First, our ministry email went down (thankfully a friend notified us so we could get it corrected) and second, our ministry couple that we were going to meet messaged us that they were notified that a substantial amount of money wasn't available to them as they had originally thought. Since they were planning on paying all in-country expenses for us, this was a big deal. On Sunday, March 3rd, shortly before leaving, we had two people stop by the house with checks to cover expenses related to the trip. We also received emails about a couple of online donations that weren't expected. We had been praying specifically for these provisions and, without asking people, the Lord answered our prayers!

In January, we had blocked March 4th to 19th. We were a little off in the final bookings as we will be returning to COS on March 21st. I guess the Lord has something extra for us to do in Bangladesh those two additional days.

We write this narrative as we are flying between Dallas and Doha. With all that the Lord did to make this trip happen, what incredible things are we going to get to walk through the couple weeks we are there?

Originally posted on www.bluefirelegacy.org by Mark & Dallas Henslee on 03/08/19

Blue Fire Legacy was founded by Mark and Dallas Henslee to equip the Body of Christ to live in fullness of purity and power. Additionally, the ministry serves struggling and hurting ministers, missionaries, and their families.

To schedule speaking and training engagements or to request other services, please contact: info@bluefirelegacy.org.

To be added to our e-newsletter and/or direct blog distribution list, please visit our website at the address below.

Blue Fire Legacy
P.O. Box 1557
Westcliffe, CO 81252

www.bluefirelegacy.org

Also Available

GET YOUR COPY TODAY

Many of our clients and readers are surprised at how much they needed this material. Don't miss out on your opportunity to walk in freedom.

www.bluefirelegacy.org/resources

Especially for children

Spend an afternoon with JennyLyne learning about forgiveness. 34 page full color children's book

Order at www.bluefirelegacy.org

Also Available

GET YOUR COPY TODAY

Love and forgiveness are powerful against Satan and his schemes. This book provides a basic understanding of the spirit war you were born into and your role in the battle.

www.bluefirelegacy.org/resources

www.ingramcontent.com/pod-product-compliance
Lightning Source LLC
Chambersburg PA
CBHW031137160426
43193CB00008B/165